Advance praise for **Walking on Water**

A well-written and badly needed integration of the principles of the self-esteem "movement" and Christian theology.
>**—M. Scott Peck, M.D.**
>*(The Road Less Traveled, A Different Drum)*

Walking on Water: Self-Esteem and a Journey of Faith is must reading for anyone who wants to make their life work. Until you recognize your own dignity and worth you will be going through life "with the brakes on."
>**—Kenneth Blanchard**
>Co-author, *The One-Minute Manager*

This is a generous and gentle book written by a generous and gentle man. Despite impressive academic credentials and life-long achievements, Dr. Ball confesses his—and what he believes to be all persons'—basic fear: the fear that we do not matter.

From this pit of self-discovery, he shows us a way up and out through faith, community, and giving up the need to control, know all the answers, fix everybody, and be right at all times.

This book is a gift of love filled with power and hope from our dear friend Bob Ball.
>**Thomas A. Harris, M.D.**
>**Amy Bjork Harris**
>Coauthors, *I'm OK—You're OK* and *Staying OK*

In *Walking on Water,* Dr. Ball presents a powerful antidote to the guilt-producing religion which permeates conservative circles today. Viewing biblical stories through the prism of findings on self-esteem, he brings a fresh perspective to combat that view of spirituality which assumes that ethical and religious progress is most effectively promoted, and the perils of irresponsibility are best avoided, by holding before the eyes of Seekers a vision of perfection which keeps them perpetually ashamed of themselves. Conversational in tone, Ball's book will bring a refreshing vision of what love of self really means. It should be very helpful in adult study groups.
>**Roy W. Fairchild, Ph.D.,**
>Professor Emeritus of Psychology and Spirituality
>San Francisco Theological Seminary

In this beautifully written book, Dr. Ball brings much needed clarity to the concept of self-esteem—what it is, where it comes from, and how each of us can improve it. His richest insights for me, however, were the links between self-esteem and the teachings of Christ.

Dr. Thomas Gordon, Founder
Parent Effectiveness Training

Go tell it on the mountain . . . tell everyone you meet that this is a great book. It is a book that has been desperately needed to help integrate the science and technology of building self-esteem with the spiritual walk of faith of Christianity. I highly recommend everyone read it. It will facilitate a lot of healing of old wounds inside us and among us.

Jack Canfield
President, Self-Esteem Seminars
How To Build High Self-Esteem

Bob Ball has written an extraordinary book centered on how we can best use the human experience to live a life characterized by meaning, fulfillment, achievement, and "total wellness." Poignant, insightful, a must.

Bettie B. Youngs, Ph.D., Ed.D.
The Six Vital Ingredients of Self-Esteem

Here's a book that gives hope. Every child has the longing to know that he or she matters, as does every senior citizen, plus all the populous in the middle. Bob Ball helps us find the dignity and worth we've lost or never found, and he shows us how to keep them. I hope this book sells and sells to bless and bless.

Charlie W. Shedd, D.D.
Letters to Karen and *Letters to Philip*

From his unique position as a recognized authority on self-esteem and having served many years as an ordained minister, Robert Ball has addressed the major issues regarding possible conflicts between the self-esteem movement and the tenets of the Christian faith. This book will prove to be extremely valuable for those who have such concerns, as well as for the community at large, regarding the issue of man's fear of insignificance and the universal search for meaning, dignity and worth.

Robert W. Reasoner, President
International Council for Self-Esteem

Walking on Water

Walking on Water

Self-Esteem and a Journey of Faith

Robert Ball

SCIENCE AND BEHAVIOR BOOKS, INC.
PALO ALTO, CALIFORNIA

Printed in the United States of America.

Library of Congress Card Number 92-064376

ISBN 8314-0079-X

Cover and interior design by
Gary LaRochelle/Flea Ranch Graphics

Editing by
Rain Blockley

Typesetting by
BookPrep

Printing by
Haddon-Craftsmen

CONTENTS

DEDICATION

For Kristen and Charlie Johnson,
Taylor and Kelly Malloy,
in the hope that a part of the heritage
from their grandfather,
to be passed on to the second and third generations,
will be faith, hope, and love,
and a joyful excitement in being alive,
essential ingredients of self-esteem.

ACKNOWLEDGMENTS

Every person I've ever known has influenced the writing of this book.

Again and again the memories of particular faces, thoughts, or touches have come to me as I wrote—some reaching back into my childhood, some from persons I knew only briefly. I wish had communicated my gratitude to those persons as I thought of them, but I did not; nor can I list all their names now. Many of them would be amazed that I have remembered them or that some part of who they are had continued as a part of who I am, but it is true. In my experience, that's how it works.

A smaller number of people were involved more directly in the development of my manuscript: some reading and suggesting, others listening to my thoughts, responding and encouraging. Amy Harris was especially helpful, generously giving of her time, insights, and encouragement as she read and commented on every chapter. Each of these persons has had a direct impact on some part of the text: Stacie Anfinson, Dr. Orin Borders, Dr. Roy Fairchild, Chris Gerwig, Gordon Gerwig, The Rev. Cheryl Goodman-Morris, Dr. Mark Goodman-Morris, Susie Lange, Dr. Mary Mallory, Dr.Chuck McIntyre, Dr. M. Scott Peck, Dr. Virginia Rigden, Dr. Robert Shelton, and John Williams. It is with sincere personal gratitude that I acknowledge them and the incalculable value of their contributions.

It was a blessed day for me when Rain Blockley became my editor. She has given from her experience and sensitivities to provide me with magnificent (though sometimes vexing) insights and editorial suggestions. She also offered remarkable personal patience, support, and encouragement. Both sets of gifts are intrinsic and invaluable parts of this effort.

Without the California Task Force to Promote Self-Esteem, and Personal and Social Responsibility, and my experiences as its executive director, this book would not have been written. Because of the Task Force I was given the opportunity to explore this crucial movement, to talk to its leading spokespersons, and to reflect on its meanings and applications. I will be forever grateful for these providential learning experiences and to the Task Force members who gave me their friendship and trust.

Finally, I am among those who, from personal as well as professional experience, affirm the indispensable benefits of a nurturing support-group community. The one of which I am a part is called, if we call it anything at all, the "Sunday Evening Book Study." For more than five years we have been involved in the weekly process of discussing various books but mostly sharing, listening, responding, and caring for each other. In that period of time, we have lost and gained some members. The following were members of the group at the time this manuscript was completed: Dr. Dick and Charlotte Frink, Gordon Gerwig, Lynn Hall, Dr. Tom and Amy Harris, Helen Johnson, Alice Massey, Toni Rasmussen, Dick and Donna Taylor, Carole Williams. My now-grown children and growing grandchildren are scattered all over the western United States, so these people are my immediate family. I am grateful for their love and support.

PREFACE

The self-esteem movement is riding the crest of popularity and excitement in the United States, while the mainline Christian churches are moving in an opposite direction: experiencing an erosion of authority, influence, credibility, enthusiasm, and members. Yet I am convinced these two movements share a basic, foundational commitment: to the dignity and worth of every individual human being. So why such a divergence in directions?

One prominent reason, I believe, is that the self-esteem movement consciously addresses specific ills that are causing major disruptions and grief in people's lives and in our society. It actively seeks new approaches to individual, interpersonal, and social issues. The most committed self-esteem adherents are actively at work to reduce the plagues of crime and violence, drug and alcohol abuse, teenage pregnancy, child abuse, chronic welfare dependency, and other human agonies. Because it speaks directly to these highly sensitive areas of obvious human need, the self-esteem movement is experienced as personal, practical, and helpful—offering realistic hope to people in the midst of their unrelenting pains and fears.

Most churches, on the other hand, do not enjoy so human a public image. An increasingly large segment of our society sees the church as basically irrelevant, too often concerned with parochial religious rituals and theories, and involved in endless religious arguments. The church today is not so much criticized as ignored. (Dorothy Sayers reportedly observed that whatever else they may have said about him, Jesus' enemies never accused him of being boring. It was left to his church to present him in that light.) It is here, I believe, that the self-esteem movement has a positive emphasis on humanness and sensitivity and compassion to share with the church.

Ironically, some of the most vigorous criticisms of churches today come from within their membership—and often in response to any efforts to address the gospel to society's personal and social issues. These critics are usually the same people who ridicule and oppose the self-esteem movement, and for the same reasons. They seem adamant in their determination to avoid the painful, personal introspection required by both serious discipleship to Jesus Christ and recognition of the importance of self-esteem.

Because all of us would like to find growth without pain, health without discipline, love without risk, Easter without Good Friday, the self-esteem movement is daily in danger of being trivialized by its overzealous adherents. I once heard Nathaniel Branden, one of the movement's most prominent authors and thinkers, frame a memorable description of this danger when he said, "You can't raise your self-esteem by blowing yourself a kiss in the mirror every morning."

Christian theology can provide an antidote to this terminal threat. It has access to a depth and integrity gained through many centuries of serving humanity's deepest needs across the full array of different cultures all over the world. Though forged on the anvils of rigorous philosophical thought, the stories that compose the Judeo-Christian tradition were not spun from ivory tower reflections. On the contrary, they were born out of and nurtured through thousands of years of human aspiration and suffering—of life and death, feast and famine, sickness and health, prosperity and war, success and failure. And these stories link the human dilemma to a meaning and power beyond the immediate moment, providing a reflective distance that allows the present to be seen with a spiritual perspective and hope.

My conviction is that the self-esteem movement and the church have much to share with each other, with significant benefits available to both. And this seems the time to do it. The collapse of communism and its subjugation of the individual to the collective good, a growing emphasis on cooperative learning and individual learning styles in education, the insistence of top-level business consultants that corporations *must* be sensitive to the personal needs of individual workers, the emergence of the self-esteem movement—all these strike me as tangible evidence that, in our yearnings and fears, the people of the world are ready for a deeper appreciation and implementation of the truth taught and lived out 2,000 years ago by Jesus of Nazareth.

In all that he said and did, Jesus consistently affirmed the unconditional and incomparable dignity and worth of every individual human being. This basic truth, emerging out of intensive biblical studies, became the central tenet of my 28 years as a Protestant pastor. It served as a foundation in all my preaching, teaching, pastoral work, and counseling. It is more than coincidence, I believe, that it also includes a thoroughly adequate wording of the philosophical basis for the self-esteem movement.

The second of my basic convictions has deep and consistent biblical roots also, but my awareness of it grew out of personal experiences. It evolved from my work as a pastor, through the hours and days and months I shared with other human beings in the midst of life's most painful struggles and sorrows—as well as from years of searching, sober reflections on my own life. Twelve years into my ministry, I wrote a master's thesis around what I had come to see as the single biggest deterrent to the life and fulfillment we all seek, and for which we were created. It is: **human beings are afraid— afraid they don't matter.** This fear of insignificance, as I came to understand it, is virtually identical to what we now call low self-esteem.

Our lives are enclosed in fear—the fear that we will be left helpless, destitute, abandoned, ignored—the fear that we are, finally, not wanted, not needed, insignificant, unloved. We fear that who we are is not enough. This is low self-esteem.

The links between the self-esteem movement and Christian spirituality, and the complementary insights they provide into the journey of people in all ages to be more authentically human and more fully alive, compose the roadmap for the pilgrimage of this book. The journey is undertaken in the faith that we are meant to take it and that there is somewhere to go. There is meaning. There is hope. There is love.

> People say that what we're all seeking is a meaning for life. I don't think that's what we're seeking. I think that *what we're seeking is an experience of being alive, so that our life experiences on the purely physical plane will have resonances within our inner-most being and reality, so that we actually feel the rapture of being alive.*[1]

---

[1] Joseph Campbell, *The Power of Myth* (New York: Doubleday, 1988), p. 3.

INTRODUCTION

People seem to understand instinctively that what we are now calling *low self-esteem* is an apt description of the tormenting fear going on in their lives, of what frustrates and fatigues them, holding them from the fuller life for which they long—for themselves, their family and their world. Today, as we enter the last decade of the twentieth century, the self-esteem movement is "hot"—though the need it addresses is anything but new. A year from now it may have another name. But for today this movement provides the language and focus that go to the core of the fear that is the most serious human dilemma in this or any other age.

Early in my career as a pastor I began to be aware of the massive and destructive consequences of fear in people's lives, including my own. Then I discovered that fear is a central and consistent theme in the Bible. In the creation story (Genesis 3:10), for example, in the very first recorded dialogue between God and his human creations, God asks, "Where are you?" and Adam replies, "I heard the sound of thee in the garden, *and I was afraid,* because I was naked; and I hid myself" (emphasis added).

Who of us has not hidden out of fear—hidden behind fancy words, good works, busyness, titles and reputations, or even religion? Who has not felt naked, exposed, ashamed, weak, and insignificant? The Adam and Eve story is our story. Fear is the name of our human condition. We are born into a frightening, uncontrollable world in which all kinds of things can and do happen to destroy our most precious hopes and dreams and loves. We often feel so helpless, so powerless. Where can we go to be safe? How can we feel secure?

As a pastor I began to sense that the crucial problem beneath all the other problems in the lives of the people to whom I ministered was: they were afraid. Life is difficult, painful, hard, threatening, unpredictable, disappointing. People have to cope with death, disease, accidents, unemployment, and the threat of war—while clinging to brief moments of joy in marriage and birth and friendship and nature and successes. What are we to make of this life?

The people with whom I worked wanted to be respected, responsible citizens. Most took their faith with an amazing degree of seriousness, longing to exemplify the best that their families and their church wanted them to be. They were not bad. They were afraid. Their fears chained them in an unrelenting, though often hidden, despair. Reasonable fears became the breeding ground for irrational obsessions. Though they seldom said so, and may not have been fully conscious of it themselves, these people doubted themselves more than they did God. Their fears overshadowed their highest aspirations, turning rational fears into dark anxieties and destructive behaviors.

Out of my pastoral and personal experiences, and my study of the scriptures and modern psychology, I became convinced that the controlling fear at the center of our lives is what I chose to call *the fear of insignificance.* This fear is the deepest and most pervasive barrier between us and the life and relationships for which we yearn. We have lived with this fear so constantly and for so long that most of us are seldom even aware of it. It has become our daily "reality." And yet, because of it, almost everything we do and dream and plan is a frantic but usually futile effort to prove that it is not so, to prove that we *do* matter—a quest of quiet desperation.

Very few of us, at least at any significant depth, *believe* that we matter; and try as we may, we cannot *prove* that we do. As circumstances compel us to face this dilemma, the need for faith leaves the realm of religious abstraction and becomes a practical necessity. As the non-theist psychotherapist Erich Fromm affirmed almost a half century ago, the only way to know that we matter is to believe it.

Where is this essential but elusive faith to be found? Are there personally compelling reasons to believe that the worth for which we yearn exists, or are we stuck with clinging to the impersonal structures of religious superstitions and psychological theories?

The God of the Bible has a very personal and practical understanding of our human condition. The biblical story of Jesus' birth, for example, could hardly be more contemporary in its sensitivity to the dynamics of human fear. It explains how quietly and gently God approaches his people. He comes to be with them where they are, to share their lives. In Luke 2:10, the angel's message announcing Jesus' birth was incredibly sensitive and understanding. It began with these words: "*Do not be afraid.* For behold I bring you the good news of a great joy which shall be to *all* people" (emphasis added).

The insight and appropriateness of this ancient story are really quite amazing. As evidenced by the massive, glittering extravaganzas we fashion to commemorate Jesus' birth, in the churches as well as in the commercial world, had it been left to us, we would have handled that natal event very differently. With all the electronic props and possibilities available to us, think how we would have staged the premier emergence of the eternal God into the world!

But the biblical account turns away from pomp and power. As Phillip Brooks phrased it so sensitively in his beloved Christmas carol, "How silently, how silently, the wondrous gift is given." The Christmas story affirms that God comes to his people not as an almighty and all-powerful king, but as a human being, a helpless infant, not one to be feared but to be received, trusted, and loved. Rather than scaring us into compliance, God's intention seems to be to love us into community, into cooperation with his loving purposes. Understanding the fear that controls us, God comes to us quietly and gently.

It makes perfect sense. None of us would approach a frightened child with intimidating gestures and threatening words—or would we? One of the effects of fear in our lives is to tempt us to deny our fearfulness. In a frantic effort to feel secure without admitting our vulnerability, we miss or lose sight of the Bible's careful description of the *manner* of God's approach to us, and the consistent biblical *meaning* attached to that approach. As a result, we end up distorting the loving, accepting message that is our joy and hope.

When I ask counselors to name the one most consistent source of destructive guilt and shame and humiliation in the people with whom they work, the answer I hear most often, sad to say, is organized religion: preachers, teachers, and parents who have used the words and structures of religious faith to control, to impose their will, to bolster their own faltering sense of worth and power, to deny their own fear— and all to the detriment of those needing their care.

All too often, in spite of their noble intentions, those who have the opportunity to make a major contribution in helping people create a sense of personal worth and a confidence in their ability to live actually accomplish just the opposite. It is a matter not of bad intentions but of an inability or unwillingness to acknowledge the massive impact of fear in their lives. The first fear that needs to be faced and accepted is this fear of fear itself.

Some Christians condemn the self-esteem movement as a secular effort to perform a spiritual function. This objection saddens me. As a committed member of both communities, I am convinced that the self-esteem movement has much to offer the Christian churches, assisting them to recall and focus on their own dominant message: the "good news" of the gospel of Jesus Christ. The philosophical basis of the self-esteem movement is precisely the same as the single most obvious activity of Jesus' ministry, as well as the central message of all his preaching and teaching: the unconditional and incomparable dignity and worth of every individual human being.

The self-esteem movement has a message of hope, a hope for significance, meaning, and freedom. I believe it is a real hope—the same one born in Bethlehem. This hope is the answer to our fear. In the Gospel according to Matthew (10:23–31), Jesus explained to his disciples why, in the midst of a world full of many dangers, they did not need to be afraid.

> "Are not two sparrows sold for a penny? And not one of them will fall to the ground without your Father's will. But even the hairs of your head are all numbered. *Fear not, therefore; you are of more value than many sparrows.*" [Emphasis added]

We do not need to be afraid because we matter. We are personally loved. This same hope had been described with eloquent insight by Bernie Siegel, a surgeon on the faculty of the Yale Medical School, in his massively popular best seller, *Love, Medicine and Miracles.*

> The miracles come from within. *You are not that unloved child anymore.* You can be reborn, rejecting the old messages with their consequent diseases. When you choose to love you will still have those days on which you are not all that you'd like to be. But you can learn to forgive yourself. You cannot

change your shortcomings until you accept yourself despite them.[1]

This quote occupies a prominent place in the unfolding
of the message of this book. For now I want only to call
attention to the spiritual nature of the surgeon's language: to
the references he makes to the miracles coming from within,
to being born again, to a commitment to love, to learning to
forgive, and to self-acceptance as the means for changing
one's shortcomings. We can sometimes see the truths of the
Christian gospel with greater splendor and precision, and receive them with a new ardor and conviction, when they are
packaged in something other than their traditional religious
trappings.

Convinced that the fear of insignificance occupies a
central, tormenting place in the lives of all human beings, and
that the only force truly capable of reducing that fear to the
point where life becomes manageable, possible, productive,
and fulfilling is the faith that we are loved, this book proceeds
on the assumption that the deepest longing in all of us is a
spiritual longing.

In using the word *spiritual,* I am acknowledging that the
longing is not necessarily religious. Indeed, many have found
their experience of religion to be antithetical to their personal
and spiritual needs. But to dismiss the benefits or even the
plausibility of religion is not the same as dislodging our
human need for contact with a transcendent source of meaning
and hope and love. My mentor and friend, Dr. Roy Fairchild,
called my attention to the work of psychiatrist Gerald May,
who believes our day is witnessing a release of the repression
of the spiritual side of our natures.

---

[1] Bernie Siegel, *Love, Medicine and Miracles* (New York: Harper
& Row, 1986), p. 86.

> We repress our longings when they hurt too much. Perhaps it is not surprising, then, that we do the same with our deepest longings for God. God does not always come to us in the pleasant ways we might expect, and so we repress our desire for God. ... But something that has been repressed does not really go away; it remains within us, skirting the edges of our consciousness. Every now and then it reminds us of its presence as if to say, "Remember me?" ... We may repress our longing for God, but, like the hound of heaven that it is, it haunts us.[2]

To recognize ourselves as spiritual beings is to affirm that the longings within us cannot be satisfied without some acknowledgment of, some contact with, some relationship to a transcendent power. Though I am offended by the notion that all spirituality can be enclosed within the parameters of the Christian faith, I am also limited to Christian spirituality by my own personal knowledge and experience. I write, therefore, conscious of the limitations of my own experience and desiring to be as inclusive as I can. My understanding of Jesus Christ is that his life and teachings were inherently inclusive, and my experience is that the gospel expressed in his life and death and resurrection, and proclaimed in his words, touches both the depths and the breadth of what it means to be human.

I write this book with the hope of offering the combined benefits of psychological and spiritual insights in the quest for a fuller, richer, more satisfying, more loving, more person-centered, and more community-oriented life. This quest recognizes the centrality of self-esteem and spirituality in the whole experience of being human.

---

[2] Gerald G. May, M.D., *Addiction and Grace* (San Francisco: Harper & Row, 1988), pp. 2–3. Copyright © 1988 by Gerald G. May.

CHAPTER ONE

Moments of Truth

In the protective isolation of our living rooms, we watch as the television camera moves slowly across the charred ruins of a fire-ravaged home. Without waiting for the reporter to say it, we grasp the situation immediately. The flames have destroyed a lifetime's worth of priceless, irreplaceable treasures. The mother, her arms enfolding her two children with a more-than-ordinary fervency, is herself being held in the shaky, grateful embrace of her husband. She speaks for all of them and for all humankind: "We're just thankful our family got out alive. That's all that really matters."

With the courage of imagination, even there in our living rooms, such moments allow us an experience of the truth: human beings are of unconditional and incomparable worth. Everyone knows it, and yet—to some extent and on some days more than others—none of us seems to believe it. Day by day, year after year, we go on living as if money matters, or power, or reputation, or popularity, or being right, or being religious. Pursuing these as goals proves to be disappointing and destructive, often disastrous; but it also leads, almost inevitably, to another personal experience of the ancient truth: when it's all sifted out, human beings are what matter.

Is there anything that matters more?

The universal awareness of this reality was symbolized in Alex Haley's massively popular *Roots,* when Kunta Kinte's father lifted the infant with his face to the heavens, and said softly, *Fend kiling dorong leh warranta ka iteh tee.* " ("Behold— the only thing greater than yourself.") [1]

As a parent I experienced this truth both personally and profoundly. Many times in my children's bedrooms after they were fast asleep, I'd look at those beautiful, precious, in- nocent faces and be overwhelmed with the depths of parental love—mixed up with a painful combination of regret and shame. I wanted to wake them up and say, "I love you so much, more than anything. I'm sorry I got so angry. Please, please forgive me. I want to take back the harsh and hateful words I spoke. I'm sorry it was so important to me to prove that I was right and you were wrong. I'll never do it again, never, never! You are beautiful, wonderful, precious human beings. I love you so much—more than anything else in all the world."

At such moments I felt myself near the limits of my capacity to be in touch with life's meaning. Even now, many years later, I still believe those were times when I was seeing life with the most clarity. Living, breathing, flesh-and-blood, frequently aggravating, always mysterious, human beings are what matter. This continues to be true even though such moments of insight and resolve don't last. I did get angry and yell at my kids again, sometimes the very next day. There were still times when I worked hard to prove I was right and they were wrong. I did forget how much they mattered.

Why? After those moments when the truth seems in- escapably clear, why does it keep getting distorted? Why do we forget? Why do we lose our perspective on what really matters? Most of my life I've thought it was because we are

---

[1] Alex Haley, *Roots* (New York: Doubleday, 1976), p. 3.

ultimately inadequate, bad, scarred from the moment of conception. That is what most Christians are taught to believe. Our religious tradition and our culture join together in a consensus condemnation: we are intrinsically evil.

I no longer believe that. I have never seen anyone assisted in being better, at least not for very long and never at any deep level, by believing him- or herself to be a bad and inadequate person. I know of no instance in which that negative self-understanding improved people's efforts to live as they wanted to live, or as their churches and culture wanted them to live. Getting down on myself for failing to live up to the solemn, loving resolves I made when I was seeing life and myself most clearly certainly didn't improve my ability to be the kind of father I wanted to be.

I still do bad things and say bad words, but I no longer believe it is because I am a bad person. A more accurate understanding is that I was, and to some extent still am, afraid—afraid that I don't matter. I became domineering, authoritarian, and unfair in my words and actions when my children's behavior touched the fear in me that they didn't truly respect me, the fear that I wasn't really worthy of respect, the fear that I was inadequate as a person. Behind my destructive, disruptive anger lived a distorting fear.

For example, with two adults and four children living in one house, it was evident that our home could quickly resemble a trash dump if coats and books and shoes and toys were not put away. As the father in the family, I felt it was my responsibility to maintain an orderly household, and I delivered my lecture on this subject frequently—with appropriate and, I thought, convincing explanations.

Yet many an evening when I came home for dinner, I found our family room decorated with mounds of abandoned books and coats and shoes and other adolescent paraphernalia resting wherever it had happened to land after being tossed aside. These mounds virtually hid the sprawling bodies of the four young TV-watchers who had created this homey version of modern art.

My customary response was to blow my top, reminding them one more time of the importance of orderliness and of their selfish disrespect for the welfare of the family. My outburst produced shamed and sullen children who dutifully got up and put their various possessions where they belong-ed, or at least somewhere out of sight. A second result was that the evening meal, and sometimes the whole evening, became a tense and unhappy scene for everyone. I hated being a hard-edged monster, polluting the atmosphere with the suffocating heaviness of my authoritarian harangues, but it was my job. I was the father. What else could I do?

Sometimes as I drove home from work in the evening, I'd begin getting myself prepared for the trashed-up house. I'd rehearse staying calm and giving clear but civil commands for rectifying the domestic disorder. But for all my preparations and good intentions, it didn't work. Within a few minutes I'd lose my temper and the angry, sullen scene would repeat.

Finally, painfully, a new understanding came my way; and this new understanding *did* make the situation different. The new insight was this: I'd been delivering frequent and emphatic lectures about how things were supposed to be around the house, but my explicit directions were consistently ignored. That lack of response triggered in me a longstanding fear that I wasn't being taken seriously as a father, or even as a human being. So, out of my fear, my fear of insignificance, I responded with anger, demanding what can never be gotten by demand: respect for my authority and for me as a person. As a result, I came off sounding like, "Kneel, you slaves!" This provoked even more disrespect and resistance.

When I became aware of my fear, I saw the whole scene differently. It was not my kids' responsibility to reassure me that I was, indeed, a respected authority figure—which is what I was demanding of them. My fearfulness was *my* problem. When I acknowledged my fear, I was able to take responsibility for it and able to choose not to be controlled by it. Then I could speak to my kids clearly and even kindly. "Well, I see that all those books and coats and shoes are scattered around again. At the next commercial, let's get them put away. Okay?" The situation needing action was acknowledged, but no one was demeaned or accused of being an incompetent or bad person. The mess was cleaned up, and we were able to have a happy, mutually respectful meal and evening.

The reason I couldn't hold on to the precious truth about the unconditional and incomparable worth of my kids is that, for all my intellectual assents about human worth, I didn't believe it—*about myself. I was afraid that I didn't matter.* This is a point most of us miss: our conviction concerning the incomparable worth of persons has no authenticity unless we matter to ourselves. If persons matter, you matter. You are a person. So am I.

I had paid lip service to various philosophical propositions about human worth, but my true attitudes were ambivalent and contradictory. I valued myself and others only in part—only for our admirable qualities. Then I got in touch with what was a major part of my core belief: that I was bad: weak, unworthy, and unlovable. This negativeness was not in my immediate consciousness, but it was the controlling conviction at the deepest place in my being. As a result, even though I was not consciously aware of it, I was working hard to prove it was not so: to prove that I was strong, smart, capable, and worthy of love. Controlled by this compulsive need to prove my worth, my actions—such as those with my kids— betrayed what I didn't want to see or admit. Beneath all my authoritarianism and in spite of my accomplishments, I was a prisoner to my deep sense of personal insignificance.

I had convinced myself that handing out all those angry, harsh, demeaning, self-justifying words was my proper role and responsibility as a father. It was the way my father had treated me, and he was a devout Christian, a committed husband, a respected educator, a hard-working and honored member of the community. Besides being dominating and authoritarian, he often did some very nice and helpful things for me and for others. I'm sure he loved me the best he could, in the best way he knew. And he was my father, my role model.

My father was highly respected by the community. I certainly was aware of that, and I respected him too—but my respect was more like fear. Somewhere in my childhood and adolescent consciousness I sensed that I had to please him to survive. I feared him and his severe condemnations. Sometimes, secretly, I dared to hate him. But always I yearned for his acceptance and approval. I know now I really wanted his love; but at the time, acceptance and approval were as much as I could dare to hope for. Much as I hated it, I had accepted that he was right—which meant I was wrong, not just in my behavior, but wrong as a human being.

Without being conscious of it, I thus allowed my life to be controlled by my fear of insignificance. Most all my thoughts and actions were frantic efforts to prove I was not what my interpretations of my father's words and actions had convinced me I was; wrong, weak, unworthy, naughty, selfish, unlovable. I feel sure he had no intention of saddling me with a controlling fear of insignificance, no more than I wanted that for my children; and yet, to some extent or another, in both cases, that's what happened.

Believing such things about myself was so painfully unacceptable that I pushed those horrendous fears as far from my consciousness as I could. I worked very, very hard (another trait I picked up from my father) to prove that such thoughts were not so—even though I was deeply convinced that they were. And how could I prove they were not? The same way my father had done and for the same reasons: by showing myself stronger, smarter, and more powerful than the people around me, who were often my kids. This meant I had to make it clear to them that they were wrong, weak, unworthy, naughty, selfish, and unlovable. That wasn't all I taught them, and it wasn't at all what I intended to teach them; but that's what happened.

What I did to my kids was demeaning and destructive, an example of the biblical adage that the sins of the fathers are visited on their children to the second and third generations. I agonize over (and have asked their forgiveness for) the pain it has caused them—and me—but I didn't do it because I was bad. I did it because I was afraid, afraid that I didn't matter, afraid to let them know how afraid I was. I allowed those fears to control me. Out of fear, I acted in ways that were painfully destructive to the people I loved as well as to myself. I allowed those fears to blind me to the truth.

THE TRIUMPH OF THE INDIVIDUAL

Human beings are of unconditional and incomparable worth. We all affirm it, but we don't believe it, especially not about ourselves. We want to matter. That need is unrelenting within us because the truth of the universe is that we *do* matter. To matter and to know it and to live it are our birthright, our authenticity, our hope. More than anything else in the world, we want to matter—and we do. But we fear that we do not. So we spend our lives in the futility of trying to prove something that is already true but that we don't really believe. Furthermore, the reality that we matter is something that cannot be proven. It is, finally, a matter of faith. The only way to know that we matter is to believe that we are capable and loved. What I felt when I looked at my sleeping kids is a reflection of eternal truth, a breakthrough from the world of fear to the world of love. Those experiences were small, recurring reminders of the way God feels about every human being in the whole world. The "good news" of the gospel is that God loves and values every person in the world. We are all unconditionally and eternally loved and precious to God— capable, needed, important, forgiven, valued, wanted.

According to the biblical account, communicating this message to all the people in the world is so important that, in Jesus Christ, our Creator willingly laid down every perk connected with being God: his reputation, his rights, his honor, his dignity, his power, his authority, his immunity from pain. God counted all of his honor and dignity and rights as unimportant in comparison to what is ultimately important: the truth—the unconditional and incomparable dignity and worth of every individual human being. This is the biblical story.

John the Baptist intuitively recognized Jesus as the long-awaited Messiah when he came to the Jordan River to be baptized. But later, as Jesus got into his ministry, John began to question his own perception. Jesus wasn't using his divine powers to punish wicked sinners, as John had been sure he would. After John was imprisoned by King Herod, he sent his disciples to ask Jesus if he was in fact the Messiah, or should they be looking for another. In John 7:22, Jesus gave the messengers this answer to take back to John:

> Go and tell John what you have seen and heard: the blind receive their sight, the lame walk, lepers are cleansed, and the deaf hear, the dead are raised up, the poor have good news preached to them.

What an amazing response! Not at all what we might have expected. So surprising that we're apt to miss the message still. *Jesus chose to verify his authenticity by pointing to the care he was giving to human beings in need.* Nowhere in his response did he mention any religious proofs. He knew John would recognize the words he quoted as coming from the writings of the prophet Isaiah—prophesies that anticipated the work of the Messiah. But of the many messianic passages available, Jesus chose one that focused squarely on the importance of human beings. Jesus wanted it clearly understood that the work of God in the world is the work of promoting and preserving the dignity and worth of every individual human person.

Many of us who have spent years in Christian churches, in precisely the spot where the Christian gospel should reasonably be expected to be heard, and have never gotten close to hearing that message. In fact, what many of us have received in those churches is precisely the opposite: that we are wrong and weak and unworthy and naughty and selfish and unlovable.

John Bradshaw gives us a classic picture of this problem. Reporting on his days in a parochial elementary school, Bradshaw explains that the instructor/priest would line his students up on the playground to receive their grade cards. The cards with Fs he threw down on the ground. The youngsters to whom they belonged were forced to get on their hands and knees in front of their classmates in an act of humiliation to retrieve the messages of their failure and shame.

Perhaps, you say, the priest accomplished what he set out to do. Bradshaw admits he was motivated to be an achiever to avoid the humiliation of groveling in the dirt for his report card. But at what cost? When a "man of God" humiliates and ridicules God's children for their failures to achieve certain academic standards, or anything else for that matter, what message is conveyed to them about God and about themselves? What message is communicated about God's regard for the dignity and worth of being human?

Even if we have been spared such demeaning treatment, what message is given to us when we witness it happening to other human beings? Much that is accepted as traditional religious practice has the effect of alerting us to be ever on guard—warning that if we fail to measure up to the standards

set by those in authority, we too will be cast down as unworthy, unwanted, unimportant failures deserving of public
humiliation. The essential gospel message that every individual human being is precious and important and loved is
more than lost. It is deeply and aggressively contradicted.
Things cannot be different until we acknowledge that this
contradiction exists.

Throughout history, in the name of God and love and
freedom, the words and structures of religion have often been
used as a refuge for the deeply ingrained fears of those in
positions of power. With the name and authority of the church
as their justification, such leaders simply hide from their own
fears of insignificance, of a life that seems to make no difference in the world or in time or in the lives of others. In
biblical days, Jesus was constantly in conflict with people in
positions of religious and political authority. Almost daily he
was assaulted with trap questions from the religious leaders,
the scribes and Pharisees, who hoped to catch him in some
violation of the sacred law. Finally, it was the political authority of the Roman government, acceding to the demands of the
religious leaders, that had him crucified. Rather than seeking
to accommodate to and share in the prestige and power of
recognized leaders, which he could easily have done, Jesus
consistently stood up for the outcasts, the disenfranchised,
those who were labeled sinners. It was among these groups
that he found most of his friends and followers. Jesus never
deserted his commitment to the unconditional, incomparable
worth of being human.

The two-thousand-year history of the Christian church
provides endless examples of frightened people manipulating
their faith and their fellow human beings in spectacular, ego-
stroking crusades. These recognized shames in the church's
history were the products of unrecognized and unresolved
fear. By these outer efforts, leaders sought to prove to the
world and to themselves that their inner sense of insignificance was not warranted.

Yet, in the Bible and throughout the history of the church, something else has been persistently at work also: the truth. The Protestant Reformation in the sixteenth century is but one conspicuous example of life's deepest truth breaking free from its confinement in the dogmatic dungeons of human fear. For centuries the power of the church in Rome had been a dominant influence in Europe's economic and political life. To maintain control over the masses, religious leaders wielded the threat of eternal damnation. With fear as their primary weapon, church authorities and political leaders combined in an uneasy and unholy alliance to maintain their own powers at the expense of the dignity and freedom and worth of those subject to their control.

Historians cite October 31, 1517, as the day the Reformation began. On that day an Augustinian monk by the name of Martin Luther nailed his 95 theses to the chapel door at Wittenburg, Germany, challenging the Pope to a debate. On that day the lines were drawn, sides began to be chosen, and the theological war was formally declared; but the underground currents for reform had been cascading about in the depths of the human psyche for as long as the dignity and worth of human beings had been assaulted and denied. Unaware of the immensity of what he was doing, Luther opened the gates to a long-suppressed flood of anger and fear and the longing for freedom and respect.

The key phrase of the Reformation reveals that human worth was precisely the central issue. That phrase, "justification by faith," means that people cannot attain salvation or fulfillment or whatever it is that life has to offer by any merit or goodness they can attain. People do not gain spiritual goals by any material abundance or personal achievements, no matter how devoutly religious their efforts may be. The only way people can find God and truth and life and meaning and hope—salvation—is to be "justified by faith alone." That is, they find salvation *by believing themselves to be loved by God.*

Living by faith, which is the condition for being human, is infinitely difficult—*because we are afraid we are not loved.* Ironically, even within the lifetimes of the principal reformers such as Luther, their followers began creating new rules of acceptability, new confessions of faith, and new rules of behavior for determining who was in and who was out. And to this day, the debate between the advocates of faith and the advocates of good works continues virtually unabated. On the one hand, it is reasonable to expect deeds of compassion and understanding and love from those who fully believe them-selves to be loved. Jesus himself said, "By their works you shall know them." On the other hand, the whole message of the gospel is that those beneficent deeds are the result of believing ourselves to be loved and not the prerequisite for it. "We love *because* he first loved us" (I John 4:19, emphasis added). How sad but common it is to see people with low self-esteem slaving to be useful and helpful, attempting to gain through good works the positive sense of themselves they yearn for but do not believe.

There are many ways to distort and deny the truth of the unconditional and incomparable worth of human beings. In the church as well as everywhere else, those who fear for their own worth (perhaps all of us) attack that truth in various ways. But because it is the truth, it cannot be destroyed. In spite of our fears, it keeps reappearing. Today it has become a roaring ocean.

In their thoughtfully considered and widely read fore-cast for the last decade of the twentieth century, *Megatrends 2000,* Naisbitt and Aburdene speak of a major trend at work in our world and call it "the thread connecting every trend described in this book":

> The triumph of the individual signals the demise of the collective. Even Communists are persuaded that only the individual creates wealth. President Gorbachev has said that what was required for the

> Soviet Union was a new "individual-based social-
> ism." Unions concede that people must be rewarded
> for their individual efforts. . . . Within all collective
> structures—organized religion, unions, the Com-
> munist party, big business, political parties, cities,
> government—there is a possibility of hiding from
> one's individual responsibility. At the level of the
> individual that possibility does not exist. There is
> no place to hide. [2]

This is not to say that the worth of each human being has
only recently become important. It always has been so, but
the economics of today's marketplace are bringing a unique
emphasis to individual creativity and judgment over obedi-
ence and brawn. This renewed recognition of the worth of the
individual is simply the most recent expression of that which
has always been true. Today we are beginning to appreciate
that importance in urgent and compelling new ways.

People in the United States have been consciously
aware of the dignity and worth of every individual human
personality since before 1776, when our Declaration of
Independence proclaimed that every person is endowed by
the Creator with inalienable rights to life, liberty, and the
pursuit of happiness. Yet, it was nearly a century later, after
the devastations of a bloody civil war, that our society's philosophical assent to the universality of human worth began to
recognize that black human beings belong within that declaration also. Even though it seems incredible to us today, it was
still another half-century after that, and after another vicious
struggle, before female humans achieved recognition as being
qualified to participate in the political process.

---

[2] John Naisbitt and Patricia Aburdene, *Megatrends 2000* (New
York: William Morrow, 1990), p. 299.

Still today various minority groups continue marching, demanding recognition of their status and equality as human beings. Recognized medical researchers recently came forward with data giving possible support to the notion that gay men received their sexual orientation genetically. Immediately, prominent pastors in the city where I live were quoted in the newspaper and on television, dismissing these new findings as bunk and insisting that certain biblical "proofs" took precedence over any scientific research. One is reminded of the church's repudiation of Galileo. No wonder so many question the church's commitment to the basic thrust of Jesus' ministry: the dignity and worth of every individual human being.

We should not be surprised that the contemporary, popular self-esteem movement is grounded in an ancient truth. Knowing and even accepting a truth intellectually are not the same as implementing it in our lives or society. That, obviously and painfully, takes some time; and that is why the self-esteem movement is so important to us today.

One reason that implementing what we understand to be true takes a long time is that—yes, you guessed it—we are afraid. Change can be terribly frightening. We cling to existing religious and political and psychological structures because we are afraid, and because, though intimidating, those structures also seem to afford us a measure of security. Within their familiarity, we can hide from the reality that we are not so big and strong and in control of everything as we would like to believe. By not questioning and not examining the structures in which we live, even if they are demeaning, we don't have to face up to our pain. We fear change because it rips away the superficial protection of the adaptations we have made, revealing our fears to us and to those around us.

Racial prejudice is an example. Prejudice is born out of fear. The structures of racial prejudice are maintained to demonstrate that the majority race "matters" and the minority race(s) do not, or at least not as much. Members of the majority race typically want to maintain the status quo, not only for fear of losing their privileges but also for fear of facing up to the fragile idiocy on which their sense of worth is built: that their race is superior to other races. To lose that, they fear, would be to lose everything. This simply reveals the depth of their fear that, in fact and in themselves, they have nothing that gives them a sense of worth. Prejudice is an expression of low self-esteem.

To let go of prejudices, convictions, or behaviors that have been long-time securities leaves us temporarily adrift, in chaos, frantically striving to reestablish our sense of direction and order. This is a frightening and painful transition. But changing course is essential if we find ourselves headed in the wrong direction.

What is the basis for claiming that human beings are of unconditional and incomparable worth? Where does that ultimate importance come from? On those dark nights of the soul, when we cry out to know if there is any hope for us, to whom do we cry? If there is hope, whence does it come?

Our worth as human beings does not come from what we produce or achieve, though that is the controlling assumption of Western society. If human worth came from achievements, then being human would not be of unconditional and incomparable worth. Those who achieved the most would matter more than those who achieved less. The same would be true if we measured human worth on the basis of race, sex, intelligence, good looks, popularity, athletic ability, philosophy, religion, sexual orientation, health, height, or charm.

So where does human worth come from? The writers of the Declaration of Independence said what the Bible says: that it comes from God: "endowed by our Creator." Scary as that is, I don't see any way around it. It's scary because it means our worth is completely out of our control. It's scary because we can't prove it. We can't show that we matter more than someone else, no matter how much we may want to or how hard we work to prove that we do. It's scary because our only access to that worth is through faith, through belief.

It is scary because it forces us into a face-to-face frontation with the idea that human beings are utterly dependent on God for everything: their lives, their meaning, their hope, their sense of worth. This is central to Christian spirituality, but it is not simply a religious argument.

> Everyone who is seriously involved in the pursuit of science becomes convinced that a Spirit is manifest in the Laws of the Universe—a Spirit vastly superior to that of man, and one in the face of which we, with our modest powers, must feel humble.[3]

We can feel humble and, at the same time, of great worth. The good news of the Christian gospel is that that "vastly superior" Spirit loves us, a position reflected in most all of the great world religions. Barbara Marx Hubbard, who in 1968 published *The Center Letter* with statements concerning the future from such leaders as Abraham Maslow, Lewis Mumford, and Thomas Merton, sees all the world's religions preparing us for this new understanding.

> The great yogis, the Hindu religion, the Buddhists, and the Muslims all predicted and prepared us for this transformation. I envision not just an ecumenical joining of the religions, but rather a fulfillment of the vision of all the religions, with the Old and New Testaments being evolutionary components of our spiritual relationship with God.[4]

---

[3] Albert Einstein, quoted in *Noetic Sciences Review* (Sausalito, CA: Institute of Noetic Sciences, Midwinter, 1990), page 3.
[4] Barbara Marx Hubbard, "God as Global Love," in *For the Love of God* (San Rafael, CA: New World Library, 1990), p. 82.

CHAPTER TWO

What Is Self-Esteem?

Impeccably fashionable and exuding an intimidating aura of arrogance, "Arthur" enters a room and everyone knows he is there. He is clearly and confidently in control. Self-assurance flows from every classic gesture and aristocratic inflection. Introduced as an expert on a particular subject, Arthur quickly and modestly denies it—and then spends the next hour giving example after example to demonstrate that indeed he is. His polysyllabic monologue, as close as he can come to a conversation, is framed by his neatly trimmed beard and consistently establishes new levels of flowery eloquence. To be in his presence is to have the distinct sense of encountering a modern-day Cicero or a walking academic dictionary.

Arthur's masterful smile and incredible self-confidence are precisely the images which, for many people, jump to mind when they hear the term *self-esteem*. It's crucially important to know: *that's not it!*

For all his apparent buoyancy and glad-handing charm, my experiences with Arthur over an extended period revealed him to be a profoundly lonely person with a deeply troubled spirit. I thought of Arthur while reading Jesus' description of some people in ancient Palestine (Matthew 23:27):

> . . . you are like whitewashed tombs, which out-wardly appear beautiful, but within they are full of dead men's bones and all uncleanness.

What graphic, accurate imagery: beautiful but dead, bones without being or meaning. Arthur, and the people about whom Jesus was speaking, would like very much to convince the rest of the world (and themselves) that they are totally in charge, in control. They're not. I recall that as a freshman at a large university I was smitten by the suave assurance of the seniors. They seemed to have tapped into an endless supply of premium quality self-esteem, but by the time I got to be a senior I had learned their secret. *They fake it!*

So exactly what, then, is self-esteem? **Self-esteem is a deeply personal and pervasively controlling decision, a value judgment, that each of us makes about his or her own competence and worth as a person.**

What Arthur has is the opposite of healthy self-esteem. It's called *narcissism.* Narcissistic people appear to the world to have super-inflated egos, as if they prize themselves consistently and without question; but, in fact, the opposite is true. In a "think tank" conducted by the California Self-Esteem Task Force in San Francisco in May 1988, Dr. M. Scott Peck, author of *The Road Less Traveled* and one of the best known and most respected psychiatrists in the United States, responded to the charge that self-esteem and nar-cissism are the same by saying, "Self-esteem is not narcissism. Narcissism is a deep, personal terror." Interestingly, when I shared my admiration for the profundity of that quote with Arthur, he got very angry.

Narcissism reflects a painful inner woundedness result-ing from neglects to one's needs for love in early childhood.

The pain from not being loved during that critical, formative period causes its victims to separate themselves from the source of their pain, from the world, from reality, from life— which leaves them separated from themselves. Inside they're like "dead men's bones." Narcissists exist in their own little, lonely towers, dreaming up visions of themselves as mighty and magnificent. These are frantic but futile efforts to salve their painful longings for a love that will not desert them. Even successes do not appease them. Their longings for an authentic, personal love persist with a demanding and insatiable intensity within that dark and dreaded emptiness.

Narcissism is the most common misconception but only one of a wide range of distorted images that people associate with self-esteem. Because healthy self-esteem ranks among the most critically important qualitites to which any human can aspire, it is essential to work toward as much clarity as possible in understanding what those words really mean.

For starters, self-esteem isn't an option. Everyone exists somewhere on the self-esteem continuum, somewhere between healthy and not healthy, high and low. The next chapter takes an extended look at where self-esteem comes from. For now it is enough to note that in some condition or another, we all have it. Even when our self-esteem is low, it's still very much alive and exercising its profound and perplexing influence on every part of our lives. So it's not accurate to say, "I have no self-esteem." People who say this usually mean their sense of confidence and self-worth is very low, but low self-esteem is not the same as having no self-esteem.

Even people with healthy self-esteem don't always feel good about themselves. In their courageous integrity, they sometimes see some painful and discouraging realities in their lives and in the world around them. And yet, even on those days when they are not all they would like to be, people with healthy self-esteem do have a solid core of authenticity within them. Even on those days, they accept themselves and take responsibility for their own lives. Their judgments about themselves are their own. They are making their own decisions and living their own lives. They learn not to measure their thoughts or their actions by anyone else's expectations. They do not allow anyone else's judgment about them to determine how they feel about themselves.

This same honest, personal reflection, so necessary for responsible living, can be destructive when done by people with low self-esteem. William Temple, at one time the Archbishop of Canterbury and a man who had no great admiration for what he saw of the psychology being practiced in his day, discouraged people from spending much time looking into themselves. He saw, correctly, how relentless introspection can consume a person's time and energy, and how often people thereby chain themselves to a morbid, self-centered preoccupation with their own faults and failings. So Temple wisely advised that if we must go probing into ourselves, we first need to pause long enough to remember how we look to Jesus Christ.

People who have a clear picture of how they look to Jesus—loved, forgiven, accepted, prized—can look into themselves with a helpful kind of honesty. They can rejoice at their strengths without false humility or embarrassment, and they can look with acceptance and understanding at those things that indeed need to be corrected or changed. The archbishop was all too aware that people who lack a deep, positive self-regard usually condemn themselves before they even begin their inward journey. Whatever they find within them that doesn't meet their unrealistic standards of acceptance frightens and shames them so that they cannot see those qualities and behaviors for what they are. The results of this distortion are greater self-alienation and, frequently, a preemptive writing off of some of their actual strengths as if they were faults and weaknesses. Carl Jung insisted that the *shadow,* which was his name for that part of ourselves we judge as unacceptable, "is ninety percent pure gold."

Just as people with healthy self-esteem do not always feel good about themselves, nor are they defeated by painful experiences or behavior that is less than what they themselves would want. Their fundamental faith in their own worth allows them to reassess themselves accurately, to design more effective strategies, and to turn adversity and mistakes into growth and gain.

A prominent characteristic of narcissistic people is that they are forever and frantically competing with the people around them, attempting to prove a superiority that even they doubt (though they may have succeeded in blocking the awareness of those painful doubts from their own consciousness). Healthy self-esteem has an exactly opposite effect. The higher a person's self-esteem, the more sensitivity and caring he or she has to share with the rest of humanity. Having an authentic sense of their own worth, people with healthy self-esteem do not need to win victories over others to gain confidence in themselves or to affirm their place in the world. Their sense of their own worth allows them to be compassionately sensitive and supportive to other people.

In my own life, the people who have been the most genuinely encouraging and helpful are, without exception, people who prize and value themselves. They include several teachers, a pastor in an incredibly small church who drove his old car all over western Kansas because he truly cared about kids, a woman dying of cancer (who lived much longer than the doctors ever imagined she would), the CEO of a newspaper company, and a few personal friends. The people with whom we experience the highest level of comfort, who threaten us the least, who encourage us the most, are people who have a genuinely positive sense of their own worth and competence as human beings. This releases them to be personally and supportively present to us.

Another common misconception is to think of self-esteem as the status we gain from external images, social standing, and public reputation. If we allow our sense of ourselves to be controlled by the opinions and judgments of others, then we end up with an image of ourselves that is not actually *self*-esteem at all. In that situation we think so poorly of ourselves that we have allowed other people to take charge of deciding our worth. We have chosen to disengage our responsibility for choosing, abandoning responsibility for our own self-esteem and replacing it with what I call *other-esteem.*

Inevitably, inescapably, other people's responses *do* have an impact on our lives. That can't be avoided. Allowing those external messages to control our sense of ourselves differs from that, however. It means abdicating our existence as unique and responsible human beings. The chances are that as we look deeply into ourselves, the more painfully obvious it becomes that in a desperate effort to be loved or at least approved by those around us, we too easily accept their judgments about us as our own. When we allow this to happen, we have surrendered our real identity, our substance, our souls, our sense of ourselves as independent and worthwhile human beings.

Painful though it may be, we need to recognize and acknowledge the extent to which we allow the judgments of others to control our images of ourselves. That is the first and necessary step in the process of reclaiming that crucial responsibility for ourselves. As adults, our self-esteem is totally our own responsibility. Nathaniel Branden says it clearly.

> Self-esteem, on whatever level, is an intimate experience; it resides in the core of our being. It is what I think and feel about myself, not what someone else thinks or feels about me.[1]

---

[1] Branden, Nathaniel, *How To Raise Your Self-Esteem* (New York: Bantam, 1987), p. 8.

One last comment about what self-esteem is not. Though a sense of confidence in one's own capability and worth is a part of healthy self-esteem, self-confidence *per se* is not the same as self-esteem. Self-confidence is related to specific areas of competence, such as the ability to ride a bike, give a speech, bake a cake, write a letter, rear children, play tennis. When I'm functioning within one of my areas of skill, my self-confidence will likely be high—until someone with abilities superior to my own comes along. What happens then is one illustration of the nature of self-confidence. It is circumstantial and conditional and therefore fragile, whereas self-esteem, as we shall see, is more abiding and stable.

I experienced the vagaries of self-confidence after being a student in a relatively small high school. I had managed to gain a sense of self-confidence in my scholastic abilities. But when I went off to the big state university, my self-confidence was replaced with feelings of inadequacy and inferiority—even before I attended my first class. The stories I'd heard about the concentration of "brains" at the university played on my fears and my less than robust self-esteem, convincing me I was out of my league.

The self-confidence that served me well in high school evaporated, with predictable results. For two years I struggled. Slowly and painfully, supported by a growing familiarity with the college setting and one fortuitous happenstance, I began to regain some of my self-confidence as a student. This renewed self-confidence also had a positive influence on my self-esteem, my sense of myself as a worthy and capable human being. As a result, my grades immediately improved. This is but another indication of how deeply our behavior and successes are ruled by our images of ourselves.

My high school self-confidence as an athlete, on the other hand, never returned. I did not have university-level abilities. Over the years since, as my physical strength and coordination have gradually declined, my self-confidence as a tennis player has declined also. This shows the transitory nature of self-confidence, and that's why it's important to distinguish it from self-esteem. Even though my confidence in my skills as a tennis player erodes with age, I enjoy playing tennis as much as or more than ever before—because declining abilities do not erode my sense of worth, my self-esteem, my joy in being alive.

Self-esteem is not narcissism or other-esteem or self-confidence. **It is a deeply personal and pervasively controlling decision, a value judgment, that each of us makes about his or her own competence and worth as a person.**

OUR DECISION

Most people find it hard to think of self-esteem as a decision because they don't remember ever having made it. The first self-esteem decision we make is a precognitive decision, that is, it is made in early childhood when we're not conscious of deciding anything at all. Nevertheless, virtually all authorities in child development now agree, as Erik Erikson theorized in the 1950s, that specific, persisting attitudes do come into being in our lives as infants and children. For instance, Erikson became convinced that we establish our basic sense of trust or mistrust in the first six to twelve months of life. Without some other experience that equals the emotional significance of the infant's first year, our basic sense of trust remains unchanged for the rest of our lives.

So too with self-esteem. Based on our experiences in early childhood—mostly with our parents—we make a decision about our competence and worth as persons. Based on her extended and highly regarded experiences as a family therapist, Virginia Satir was convinced that the family is the birthplace of self-esteem:

> I am convinced that there are no genes to carry the
> feeling of worth. It is learned. And the family is
> where it is learned.[2]

The particular nature of that family experience is crucial, with long-term consequences; and yet, even in the very
best of family settings, a decision made in the early years of
childhood can hardly be considered adequate for the remainder
of one's life in the world as a responsible adult. The tragedy is
that most people go through the rest of their lives without
making another basic decision about who they are. Many,
many adults continue to function in the world with a sense of
themselves that was reasonably accurate in their infancy. At
that time they experienced themselves as small, awkward,
dependent, incompetent, powerless, lacking knowledge, and
(as they were often told) usually wrong. For functioning
adults, that self-image is both distorted and destructive.

Because we've lived with our precognitive decision so
long—for as long as we can remember—the sense of self-
worth it creates registers inside us as if it were "reality,"
God's own truth. We neither recall nor experience it as a
decision we made as infants in the midst of circumstances
that no longer exist. And yet, unacknowledged, that childhood decision continues to shape every other decision, am-
bition, and relationship throughout our lives. It reigns within
us as the only reality we've ever known about ourselves.

Many people have said to me, "Look, I'm a healthy,
successful human being with a lovely family and a fine home.
Why do I feel so crummy about myself? Why don't I have
higher self-esteem?" An important part of the answer to those
questions, for most of us, is that the present, here-and-now
realities are not being allowed to challenge and change that
early childhood sense of worth and competence.

---

[2] Virginia Satir, *Peoplemaking* (Palo Alto, CA: Science & Behavior
Books, 1972), p. 24.

Arthur is an example. He has a brilliant mind, a natural charm, and is an unusually gifted athlete; but the deep inner conviction that commands his life was made in the substance-abusive family in which he was reared. In that situation he decided he wasn't important, didn't count, and wasn't truly respected. He still spends his adult energies in a frantic but futile effort to prove that all those negative beliefs about himself are not so. Maintaining his apparently inflated sense of himself results in ever-increasing stress and separation in his life and in his relationships. Unaware, he stays stuck with that early decision as if it were still true.

Other people may exhibit exactly opposite behaviors—being shy, withdrawn, and self-deprecating—while suffering exactly the same inner feelings of being unwanted and unworthy. Self-aggrandizement and self-deprecation are different ways of responding to the same fear: the fear that we do not matter. This fear usually deafens people to the encouragement for which they long so desperately.

Have you ever tried to cheer up family members or friends? They manage to discount any evidence you present out of their here-and-now-situation, such as, "Look, you're an intelligent, caring, likeable human being." People with low self-esteem continue responding to the decision they made as young children. Whatever that old decision said about them is still their "reality." They say, and deeply believe, "I'm dumb and selfish and nobody really likes me."

The good news about recognizing self-esteem as a decision is that, like any decision, it can change. The bad news is that because it is a decision that lies buried so deeply within us, we cannot change it easily. Books and speakers who say you can raise your self-esteem by giving yourself a pep talk every morning, saying things like, "I am the greatest, unbeatable, and can do anything I want to do," are superficial and misleading. Raising our self-esteem requires a conscious and concerted effort—something like a long-term conversion.

Adults with healthy self-esteem have had to sort through the woundedness in their past (including what Jean Illsley Clarke calls our "uneven parenting") and acknowledge whatever distorted decisions they have made. They then have chosen to make new, more appropriate, and more realistic decisions about themselves, choosing to believe in the depths of their beings that they are personally precious and loved, and then choosing to act in the world on the basis of those new decisions. The new decisions change both their *manner* of seeing themselves and the world around them, and *what* they see.

The King James version of Proverbs 23:7 says: "As a man thinketh in his heart, so is he." The teachings of Jesus provide many fascinating examples of how our external lives are an expression of what, in our inner depths, we believe about ourselves. His "Sermon on the Mount" (chapters five through seven in the Gospel according to Matthew) provides many classic examples. Because of its profundity and beauty, this is one of the best known sections in the New Testament. It includes many familiar passages, such as the "Golden Rule," a verse that some people call "all the religion they need."

The richness of the Sermon on the Mount is often trivialized or missed because people fail to recognize its context. Too often people take these teachings to be impersonal commands that must be obeyed if one is to be accepted by God. Throughout the entire Sermon, however, Jesus' underlying assumption is that he is speaking to his disciples. All these teachings, therefore, are predicated on the assumption that they are being received by people who *already* believe themselves to be accepted by God—loved, forgiven, precious. Within this understanding, Jesus' words have an entirely different meaning. They become personal directions for reordering our new lives on the basis of the love we have already received and believed.

Take the Golden Rule, for example: "Do unto others as you would have others do unto you." If I believe myself to be loved, I will be loving. But if, on the other hand, my deep conviction is that I am an unwanted and unworthy person, my life will be controlled by the negative judgment that I deserve to be treated poorly. Then, following the Golden Rule, I will treat others poorly also—just as I think they ought to treat me. And this is exactly how it works. People who don't like themselves are negative and judgmental toward themselves—and toward other people also.

One other poignant example from the Sermon on the Mount (Matthew 5:33–37) has great meaning for me (and provided both the insight and the basis for my previous book on personal communication). Having listed various ways in which the religious people of his day took oaths to demonstrate sincerity, Jesus said, "But I say to you, Do not swear at all, ... Let what you say be simply 'Yes' or 'No'; anything more than this comes from evil."

As a kid I thought Jesus' command not to swear meant, "Don't cuss." But in this case, swearing refers to oath-taking. The whole point of taking an oath is an effort to verify one's trustworthiness. When you stop to think about it, demanding an oath assumes that without it a person's words cannot be trusted. So when a person says, "By God, I really mean it!" the unspoken message is, "Normally, I wouldn't expect you to believe me. But on this occasion I am using the name of the Almighty in the hope that now you will take me seriously." Taking oaths therefore reflects a low level of self-esteem.

"Do not swear at all" is not a command that must be obeyed to gain God's acceptance. Jesus is pointing out that his disciples are people of such integrity that they say what they mean: "yes" or "no." They trust themselves; they can be trusted. Their integrity doesn't depend on external proofs or legal rituals. It comes from deep within. It arises from their belief about themselves, from their conviction that they are loved.

People who believe themselves to be loved don't have to try to impress others or prove themselves. Their decision of faith in themselves gives them a sense of confidence and stability and personal worth, which allows them to function in the world with integrity. They believe in themselves. They can be believed. The decision to love oneself is the foundation for healthy self-esteem.

OUR COMPETENCE

The self-esteem decision we make about ourselves has two constituent parts. The first is a sense of competence, which refers to our competence to function effectively in the world. Life requires certain skills. It is not enough to wear a smile and maintain a cheerful outlook. The land will not produce a crop unless it is tilled, the seed planted, the harvest gathered. The bread needs to be baked, the well dug for water, the coat cut and sewn, the house built, the furnace stoked—all of which require skills and responsible effort, competencies necessary for effective living.

Beyond these obvious essentials, there are fundamental skills and strategies and techniques required for effective living, even in so basic a responsibility as child rearing. With today's staggering number of teenage pregnancies, we hear more and more about the pitfalls of "children rearing children." Age in itself is not a condition for successful parenting. Simply adding years to our lives doesn't necessarily add maturity. But growing up—disciplining oneself to listen, to care deeply and empathically, to choose to learn the skills of parenting—is essential for maturity. It is a choice we make. Effective parenting requires more than good intentions or doing what comes naturally.

At its deepest point, the competence part of self-esteem refers to how we assess our ability to live in a world that is forever challenging and unpredictable. People who doubt they possess that basic competence generally have low self-esteem. What a painful and lonely experience life is for them! They often lie to themselves in an effort to override their uncertainties. Trying to convince themselves that they *are* competent and in control, they often pretend that the world isn't complicated; that the difference between good and bad, truth and untruth, is obvious and simple; and that the difference is clear as a bell. Asserting and defending these black-and-white distinctions causes them to become ever more inflexible and dogmatic. It protects them from facing their needs to learn and to grow—so they don't. It also may give them the outward appearance of absolute competence, beneath which they live in a frenzy of terror while dealing inappropriately and destructively with life.

People with healthier self-esteem see the world for what it is: a place of challenge and change that can never be fully predicted, explained, or controlled. In full awareness of its many contingencies, they believe they are competent to live in such a world. Knowing that they do make mistakes and that they will grow from them, they believe they have within themselves what it takes to live effectively. The person with healthy self-esteem wakes up in the morning not knowing what that day will bring, but with the conviction that whatever happens, he or she will be able to deal with it in a responsible and effective way. This authentic zest for life is the sense of competence that is an essential part of healthy self-esteem.

Many years ago, long before I was even aware of the phrase *self-esteem*, a graduate school professor told our class, "The most appealing thing about any person is his [or her] ability to live." As the years have gone by, I've found this truth confirmed many times in the lives of people I have known. The most appealing people have a quiet assurance that whatever life may bring their way, they'll be able to handle it. They are not boastful or arrogant, nor are they timid or withdrawn from life. There is about them an enduring joy, an underlying belief that in spite of life's pain and tragedy, some fundamental meaning exists that is dependable and worthwhile. And they believe themselves to be a part of that indestructible meaning.

People like this sometimes get discouraged, but they are not defeated. I'm reminded of the words of the apostle Paul (II Corinthians 4:8, 9):

> We are afflicted in every way, but not crushed; perplexed, but not driven to despair; persecuted, but not forsaken; struck down, but not destroyed...

These are appealing, nurturing people. They do not intimidate others with their efforts to prove how righteous they are, nor do they drain people with their stories of how unfairly life has treated them. They are at ease with who they are: human beings who have sorrows and who make mistakes but who also are excited about being alive, confident of their own abilities to live and of the contribution they can make to the lives of others. These are the people from whom the rest of us receive acceptance, hope, and excitement.

The same adversities that destroy some people become the challenges that result in growth and maturity in others. It seems that it is not the trials we have to face but the manner in which we choose to face them that makes all the difference. Indeed, spiritual growth depends on adversity. I have a wise friend whose consistent comment about each new crisis is, 'Well, it will make your soul grow."

Some of the most magnificent competence I have ever seen has been in people with various disabilities. There are certain life skills they can never acquire, yet, beneath their disabilities, they reach into themselves and find a profound competence in being alive as human beings. Instead of seeing themselves as victims of their handicaps, they choose to accept themselves and their situation. They find and use their unique abilities for expressing their aliveness, such as offering a very personal and authentic compassion to their sorrowing neighbors or developing the gifts available to them to the highest possible level. Whether in spite of their disabilities or because of them, some of the people I know are unsurpassed in their capacity to communicate the worth of being alive.

One crucial part of this sense of competence is that it is *not* acquired through competitions or comparisons with others. The importance of this is especially great in societies such as ours, in which we base nearly all our judgments about ourselves on comparisons. We think of ourselves as shorter or taller, prettier or uglier, skinnier or fatter, smarter or dumber, richer or poorer, faster or slower. Our sense of well-being often rises or falls according to our comparative standing at any given moment.

Many traditional admonitions use comparisons. For instance, I've often heard people say they use this little maxim to keep themselves thankful: "I used to feel sorry for myself because I had no shoes. Then I saw a man who had no feet." But if comparisons with those without feet are what make us thankful, what happens to our thankfulness when we see a man with the most elegant shoes in the world? Comparisons do not make us thankful. They only give us temporary feeling of being either lucky or shortchanged, depending on the one or ones with whom we are comparing ourselves.

Genuine self-esteem is not based on comparisons, but on a deep sense of ourselves as persons who have what it takes to look at life honestly and to live it responsibly and appropriately. The most appealing and loving people in the world are people with high self-esteem, people who have chosen to believe in their ability to live.

OUR WORTH

The second part of our self-esteem decision involves a sense of personal worth. It is the conviction that we matter, that we deserve to be treated with dignity and respect—by others and by ourselves, perhaps especially by ourselves— for no other reason than that we are precious, unique, irreplaceable human beings.

Many Western societies teach that people matter on the basis of achievements. From earliest childhood we learn to feel good about ourselves when we measure up to what our elders expect of us. We please them by being quiet when they want us to be quiet and performing when they want us to perform. Our parents are proud of us when we make good grades, excel in sports, get the lead in the school play, or win a campus election. But how do they feel about us for who we are, independent of any successes or failures?

This same pattern follows us into adulthood. We continue to find ourselves being measured—by our job title and salary, the status of our friends, our patriotism, how well our kids perform, the clothes we wear, the car we drive, and so on. No wonder we all have trouble thinking of ourselves as being people of worth—people who matter—just because we are human beings.

If being a human being doesn't matter, what does? What is the worth of medicine or education or technology or literature or religion if they do not, in some way, make life fuller and richer and more livable for human beings? Human beings mattter, unconditionally and incomparably; and you are a human being. You matter.

Do you believe it? Do you treat yourself with dignity and respect? Are you kind to yourself? Are you willing to take the time to listen to yourself when you've had a hard day, to be accepting and understanding and forgiving when you are lonely or sad or discouraged? If you don't deserve such treatment, why not? Who does?

Answering these questions brings us to the question of where we human beings get our worth. As the previous chapter asked, where do we find a resource of consistent and unconditional meaning and hope? The Christian gospel affirms that we matter because we are loved by God. Yet many of us who have been reared in traditional religious communities and who look to God as our strength and hope find a contradictory question being raised. How are prizing and honoring ourselves different from selfishness, or are they?

To me, healthy self-esteem is a secular and contemporary wording for the self-love that the scriptures record as Jesus' most explicit command—and his gift—to all people. That this is not immediately apparent to many within the Christian faith is, I think, a clear indication of how far afield we have gone in our understanding of the gospel of Jesus Christ. In many religious people, the very mention of self-love brings on shudders of repugnance and dread. For them it represents the selfishness they've learned to shame and abhor and a gross violation of the selflessness they've been taught to treasure.

And yet, the widely esteemed nineteenth-century Danish philosopher/theologian Soren Kierkegaard spelled it out with unmistakable precision.

> If anyone, therefore, will not learn from Christianity to love **himself** in the right way, than neither can he love his neighbor. . . . To love one's self in the right way and to love one's neighbor are absolutely analogous concepts, are at bottom one and the same. . . . Hence the law is: "You shall love yourself

as you love your neighbor when you love him as yourself."[3] [Emphasis in original]

The Christian gospel has been robbed of much of its genius and power through the loss of this fundamental truth: people who do not believe in their own worth cannot be loving and respectful in their relationships with others. People who do not prize and treasure themselves cannot, with integrity, fulfill Jesus' most basic command: to "love one another as I have loved you." In our anxiety about ourselves, we do not always listen carefully to that command. Although its words are so simple and straightforward that they seem beyond misunderstanding, we have managed to do precisely that.

In our fear-induced rigidity, we have missed two vital points. First, this command describes exactly the manner in which we are to love others: *As Jesus has loved us,* that is, with forgiveness, understanding, acceptance, mercy, compassion, and the willingness to be personally present in times of deep sorrow as well as of exuberant joy. We are to love others regardless of how the world may measure their worthiness to be loved.

The second point is that to "love one another as I have loved you" means we begin the task of loving with the clear understanding and conviction of ourselves as ones who have been, and continue to be, loved. We are not forsaken orphans seeking to earn a place in the heavenly mansions. We are not miserable wretches hoping to curry the favor of a demanding despot. We are not hopelessly stuck in the sewers of our despicable unworthiness and shame. We are people who are accepted and forgiven and loved by God. From that stance,

---

[3] Soren Kierkegaard, *Kierkegaard Anthology* (Princeton University Press, 1946), p. 289.

that clear understanding of ourselves, we are able to fulfill what would otherwise be an impossible command. Jesus does not call his disciples to love until he has first given his own unconditional love to them.

How does this square with the biblical concept that we are all sinners, people who have failed to be grateful for and responsive to the love we've been given? Chapter 3 says more about that. For now, seeing ourselves as sinners only makes all the more glorious, more cause for great rejoicing, the reality that we are loved. It allows us to be all the more forgiving and magnanimous concerning the faults and failings of our fellow human beings.

Emphasizing the importance of self-esteem, a deep and abiding love and appreciation for one's self, is not a new or secular invention. It is at least as ancient and as spiritual as the gospel. It is my fervent hope that the insights of the self-esteem movement can help Christians recover this central, vital portion of their own heritage and share it with the rest of humanity as the reality in which we all live.

On the last night before his death, Jesus wrapped a towel around his waist and began to wash his disciples' feet. In spite of their three years of constant association with Jesus, hearing his teachings and being eyewitnesses to his miracles, the disciples did not understand his meaning. They were confused, frightened, and still competing with one another for positions of power and prestige. Jesus did not use this last moment with them as an opportunity to prove his power or as an occasion to harangue them for their failures. The disciples were being torn apart with fear and uncertainty. They needed the assurance of an experience of love. So Jesus loved them. He, their master, knelt before them and began to care for them in an act clearly associated with servants in their day. He washed their feet. It was not a manipulation to create guilt, but a gesture of understanding love flowing forth from his confident humility. Jesus was able to kneel before them to act as a servant without losing any of his stature or strength. In spite of the death awaiting him and the faithlessness of his disciples, Jesus was not in panic. He believed he was loved. He knew he had love to give. He gave it.

It was then, *after* his simple but dramatic act of selfless love, that Jesus gave his disciples one simple direction concerning their responsibilities, the way to the fullness of life's meaning (John 13:14): "If I then, . . . have washed your feet, you also ought to wash one another's feet."

Healthy self-esteem comes from choosing to believe we are loved and choosing to receive that love, and healthy self-esteem allows us to do what most needs to be done—to love— in the most difficult and trying (and important) of circumstances.

A dear friend, after reading an early draft of this chapter, suggested it would be helpful if I could give some examples of healthy self-love. I have thought of many, though they seem banal and prosaic compared to the depth of what I would like to describe. On the purely practical level, a mother can truly love her children only to the extent that she is conscious of her own worth and importance. Otherwise her expressions of love toward her children will be efforts to prove that she is a good mother, to gain the approval and love of her children, to work off some guilt for an imagined or real failure out of the past, or, more likely, some degree of all these combined with other unmet emotional needs.

Another example might be Christian evangelists. They can truly love the persons to whom they are presenting the gospel only to the extent that they are conscious of their own worth and importance. Otherwise their expressions of love are very likely to be manipulations, subtle or not, to gain converts and thus raise their own sense of righteousness and worth.

Perhaps the almost poetic nature of Jesus washing his disciples' feet on the last night before his own death is the most accurate and appropriate example possible. Even though his situation was clearly desperate and his own needs incontestably acute, Jesus' awareness that he was loved and would continue to be loved, no matter what, released him from the confinement of his own pains and problems. His sense of this allowed him to act in a deeply personal and helpful way on behalf of his friends. His love for them was not an act of nobility but a magnificent expression of faith. "Jesus, knowing . . . he had come from God and was going to God, rose and girded himself with a towel . . . and began to wash the disciples' feet" (John 13:4, 5). He believed he was loved. Therefore he was able to love. This is healthy self-esteem at its finest and best.

CHAPTER THREE

Where Do We Learn Self-Esteem?

Where does self-esteem come from? Is it possible that it's inherited, that to have either healthy or unhealthy self-esteem is a given part of each essential self? If we see ourselves as losers, inadequate to the pressures and demands of life, doomed to a life of failure and disappointment, were we born that way?

A strong and long-standing theology within the Christian church seems to support this point of view. The doctrine of original sin teaches that all people are born into the world as sinners: selfish, evil, disobedient to God, and destructive to their fellow human beings and themselves. This conviction has exerted a decisive influence on most traditions of Christian nurturing and Christian education for as far back as most in my generation can remember. The belief that people are basically evil helps define not only individual self-esteem but the nurturing and educational roles of the church as well. For those who subscribe to the doctrine of original sin, it is altogether consistent to see it as their duty to drive that evil out—or beat it out, scare it out, coerce it out, bribe it out, discipline it out, shame it out, or whatever may be necessary to expel it—from themselves and others. It also follows that they are expected to replace that evil with a new self, the character of which is selected and imposed by others who are, somehow, more capable of knowing and creating a godly human life.

Not all Christians believe in or hold identical interpretations of the doctrine of original sin. Indeed, an increasing number who are not willing to abandon it completely agree that it has been overemphasized and implemented in erroneous and destructive ways, a reality which seems to me to be beyond question. Dealing with other people, and ourselves, as if we were born with this negative and destructive orientation has catastrophic consequences. It also provides a breeding ground for unhealthy self-esteem.

With regard to self-esteem, what I *like* about the doctrine of original sin is that it includes all of humanity in the same needy position. Dr. James Wharton, an eminently respected Old Testament scholar and professor of homiletics at the Perkins School of Theology, told me years ago that he and a colleague had developed a two-line summary of the gospel of Jesus Christ:

> We're all in this thing together,
> and God is in this thing with us.

While Wharton understands as well as anyone that the gospel cannot be summarized in any two lines, this effort is far and away the most accurate and the most helpful of any I have ever heard or read.

This same message of inclusiveness shows prominently in words from Elizabeth O'Connor, author and staff member of the famous Church of the Savior in Washington, D.C. An interviewer asked O'Connor: "Do you think Christian people are aware that they are carrying emotional pain? Deeply wounded people are, of course. But what about the rest of us?" O'Connor responded:

> We are *all* wounded to one degree or another. We
> are wounded first by the household we grew up in.
> There are no perfect parents. Our parents have
> their own legacy of pain. Then we are wounded by
> the schools we go to, by our work places, by our
> churches—by oppressive structures.[1]

O'Connor's insights into the universality of our wound-edness also gives us a good start in responding to the question that began this chapter. Where and how we learn to esteem ourselves are rather complicated questions. Where we first learn it, on the other hand, is generally a simple and straight-forward matter. As noted earlier, Virginia Satir, a world-respected authority on families, spoke directly to the point.

> I am convinced that there are no genes to carry the
> feelings of worth. It is learned. And the family is
> where it is learned. You learned to feel high (self-
> esteem) or low (self-esteem) in the family your
> parents created. And your children are learning it
> in your family right now.[2]

As children we received the basis and foundation for our first self-esteem choice from our families. This crucially important first-half-of-the-story deserves our fullest attention. Understanding how people make their first self-esteem deci-sion is vital, not only for the sake of the children whose self-esteem is being shaped in our homes, but also for our own sakes—for those of us who, as adults, are ready to acknowl-edge and take responsibility for our own self-esteem.

---

[1] Elizabeth O'Connor, "Faces of Faith," *The Other Side* (1990), p. 20.
[2] Virginia Satir, *Peoplemaking* (Palo Alto, CA: Science & Behavior Books, 1972), p. 24.

Human life develops in the warm, soft, comfortable world of the womb—a world where the temperature is always just right, where nutrition is provided at precisely the right time, and where fetuses have wonderfully close relationships with their mothers. Leaving this veritable paradise, newborn infants are suddenly and involuntarily thrust into a dramatically different existence. Their new world is one of separation, alternations between attention and abandonment, light and dark, silence and noise, and, of course, diaper rash. It's a strange and often frightening new place.

How do infants feel about themselves in this "life after birth"? It depends on how welcome and wanted they experience themselves to be by their first hosts. Infants learn volumes about themselves through the responses they get from their parents—or whoever fills the parental role. Infants figure out who they are and what they are according to what they hear and how they're touched by those godlike people on whom they depend completely for their survival.

More than any other creatures, newborn human beings have a long period of dependency on their parents. This dependency is both physical and emotional. Studies show that even when infants are given every physical and medical support they could possibly need, they are seriously impaired and sometimes die if they do not also receive adequate personal attention and caring. When their needs are not met, the infant psyche registers that those needs must be unimportant, leaving them to believe that they must not be important either. Such is the process by which they learn how to feel about themselves.

So we shouldn't be surprised that so many adults walk around in the world today convinced that "What I need isn't important" or "Who I am doesn't matter." Their lives in the present are an expression of the self-esteem they learned and the choices they made in the families in which they were reared. The widely respected psychologist and author Sam

Keen paints a startling and specific picture of where and how our self-esteem is learned: "We first and forever (or not at all) learn our infinite worth from the look of adoration we see in our parents' eyes."[3]

I believe there is substantial evidence that the condition is not so permanently irredeemable as Keen suggests, and I argue later in this book that steps can and should be taken to raise unhealthy self-esteem. Yet Keen and others compel us to face this truth: what we learn about esteeming ourselves as children can affect the rest of our lives. Bernie Siegel, a Yale Medical School surgeon who has spent his professional life working with adults suffering from cancer and other serious illnesses, likewise concludes that "The greatest disease of mankind is a lack of love for children, leading to their psychological and sometimes even physical abuse, which predisposes those children to a hopeless/helpless attitude and to disease later in life."[4]

So what, specifically, do our children need from us if they are to avoid that "hopeless/helpless attitude"? They need to feel welcome and wanted. They need constant affirmations that we are delighted to have them as a part of our lives, a part of our world. They need to be allowed to develop confidence in both their lovability and their capability—the confidence that they are able to assess what's happening in the world around them and to choose appropriate and effective ways to deal with that world. They need us to care about them enough to find and absorb information on how children develop.

As a kid growing up on a wheat farm, I learned that a knowledge of the growing cycle is vitally important. This

---

[3] Sam Keen, *Fire in the Belly* (New York: Bantam, 1991), p. 227.
[4] Bernie Siegel, *Peace, Love and Healing* (New York: Harper & Row, 1989), p. 155.

meant knowing just when to plow the ground in preparation for the seed, when to plant in order to allow time for the right amount of growth before the first freeze, when to apply fertilizer, and when the grain was ready for harvest. The most effective and successful farmers are careful students of the stages of development in their crops, and they learn to be attentive to signs that indicate a disease or infestation is threatening the crop. Knowing, they can take appropriate steps to deal with the danger.

If it is important for farmers to understand the developmental process of their crops, how much more crucial it is for parents to be students of the developmental stages of their children. This includes knowing when to expect certain kinds of behavior, when to encourage and when to provide limits, when to intervene and when to be patient. Why do 18-month-olds repeatedly forget rules or requests? Why do two-year-olds say "No" so much, so incessantly, even to things they want to do? Parents who seek out such knowledge for themselves are able to understand, support, and respond helpfully to their children through each of the various stages of growth. Being a conscientious parent isn't enough. We also need to understand the developmental stages our children are going through so that we may assist them appropriately, or at least not get in their way.

As children grow, their brains develop in specific ways. This affects the way they perceive, understand, and behave in the world. It is important, for example, for two-year-olds to learn to say "No." They need to be encouraged to exercise choice. Many adults have trouble saying no because they were never allowed to when they were two-year-olds. But if the parents of a two-year-old do not understand that this is a developmental need, they can easily become very frustrated and even angry putting up with this constant negativism. As a matter of fact, it is sometimes pretty hard to take even if you do understand. But understanding makes a world of difference.

We respond much differently to a child if we understand that he or she is behaving in a way that is perfectly natural, even necessary, for that stage in his or her growing process. If we don't understand, we may get angry or hurt and end up blaming the child unfairly and destructively.

"Every child needs a face to mirror and affirm his or her feelings, needs, and drives."[5] That sentence reached out to me when I first read it, slipping through many years of shame and pain and longing to touch a tender wound in my psyche. Suddenly a giant portion of my pain and awkwardness had been recognized and defined. Even though I was reared by highly conscientious and caring parents, the "face to mirror and affirm" that every child needs is something I never got. Anytime my feelings, needs, and drives were different from what my parents wanted and expected from me, what I got was shame and punishment—probably just what my parents had gotten from their parents under similar circumstances.

The message was: Your feelings, needs, and drives are not OK. This got translated in me as: Who you are in your deepest self is not OK. In turn, this formed a significant portion of the basis for my decision about my self-esteem: Who I am is not OK. My parents, I'm sure, had absolutely no intention of wanting me to feel negatively about myself. On the contrary, I can recall them often encouraging me to smile, to get over any blues I might be feeling because I had so many good things going for me. They wanted me to be confident and happy; and yet, unintentionally but unerringly, they gave me strong reasons for deciding that I was naughty, unworthy, selfish, and wrong. I have experienced the consequences of that decision in painful and plaguing barriers throughout my life.

---

[5] John Bradshaw, *Healing the Shame That Binds You* (Deerfield Beach, FL: Heath Communications, 1988), p. 56.

How I wish I had understood about affirming feelings, needs, and drives when I was rearing my own kids. Besides being of enormous benefit in my efforts to help them develop healthy personalities, knowing that it was beneficial to mirror and affirm the deeply personal parts of their personalities would have allowed us to have a lot more fun together. Giving children that kind of respect allows them to learn how to respect themselves as they make their way through the various stages of the growing process.

Can you look back on your life and remember a particular parent or teacher or coach whom you experienced as "being there" for you? Can you remember how you responded to that person? Understanding and support are the bases for guiding children rather than attempting to rule them. The easiest way to control anyone is to rule by inconsistency, using both fear and love. While serving as a survival intelligence officer in the U.S. Air Force Strategic Air Command, I learned that alternating fear and kindness was one of the most highly sophisticated tortures used against our captured troops during the Korean War. Whether in a prison camp or in a home, this is a strong and effective way to condition someone's behavior. It also instills high anxiety and destroys self-worth.

A colleague of mine, Dr. Jane Nelsen, who has written some excellent books on positive discipline and child rearing, asks a profound and penetrating question: "Where did we ever get the crazy idea that to make children DO better, first we had to make them feel worse?" Most parents want their kids to go off to school feeling confident in their abilities to study, learn, make good decisions, and have friends. What makes us think we can prepare them for such a positive experience by telling them how bad they are, how disappointed we are in them, how selfish and ungrateful they are? Or by asking them, "Aren't you ever going to grow up? How many times do I have to tell you in order to get something through that thick skull of yours? Aren't you ashamed of yourself?"

If we really don't want to destroy our kids' self-confidence, why do we talk to them in destructive ways? Prominent among the reasons, I think, is our low self-esteem. We want to do the best job we possibly can, and when things aren't going the way we want them to, we fear we're doing a terrible job. The whole situation suddenly seems out of control, and our kids seem headed toward all those dreadful qualities we fear most. We fear that it will be evident to the whole world that we are bad parents. So we do what was done to us by our fearful parents. We try to use force or fear to control the situation and our kids, which only increases our children's anxieties and resistence.

Attempting to bolster our kids' self-confidence by giving them exaggerated praise—just the opposite of blame and shame—doesn't work either. Healthy self-esteem is not created when a mother receives the picture brought home by her kindergartner and says, "This is the most beautiful picture in the whole world!" or when a father says, "There's not another kid in America who can throw the ball or roller skate as fast as mine!" Kids know these exaggerations are not true, and the thinking/feeling process inside of them often goes something like this: "I must really be a nerd if my folks have to work that hard to find something good to say about me."

Why can't we be honest? Why can't we say, "I am delighted with your picture. I'm so pleased you brought it to me. I like what you draw. I'm going to put it on my wall." And why can't we say, "You really throw the ball well. I enjoy playing catch with you. I'm pleased when I see you take off on your skates. I'm proud that you're learning to handle them so well." Why can't we? Because of our own low self-esteem. It doesn't feel safe to us to be "who we are." It's not enough because we fear that we're not enough. We feel we have to be more than that. So we exaggerate, and our exaggerations perpetuate and compound the problem.

This is not an effort to assign blame. My intent here is to gain understanding, not to bash parents. Only with understanding are we able to take personal responsibility for our lives and make good decisions about our own growth. Most all of us have some degree of good health, and the ability to get and keep a job, to read and write and do at least simple math, to drive a car. We have not been totally destroyed by the families in which we were reared. In fact, one of the first writers to begin dealing with self-esteem issues, Jean Illsley Clarke, refuses to use the currently in-vogue phrase "dysfunctional families." She says that term makes it sound as if everything that's happened to us is bad, which obviously isn't so.

Clarke instead uses the term "uneven parenting," which suggests that there were some places along the way in our development when the parenting we received was not adequate. We need to be aware of those places of neglect or abuse and then take appropriate steps to get now what we missed then. So the point in assessing the experiences we went through as kids is not to lay blame on our parents, but to find those places where we missed what was needed. This allows us to take responsibility for getting those needs met now, which is called *reparenting*. "Growing up again and again is getting what we missed earlier so we don't have to go on living without what we need now. We grow up again so we can do better parenting, so we can feel more alive."[6]

When, for example, it became evident to me that my parents had not mirrored and affirmed my feelings, needs, and drives as I needed them to do during my childhood, it became my responsibility to find those crucial affirmations elsewhere. We can do the reparenting ourselves or we can find others (friends or therapists) who will assist us with the process. Reading books can alert us to our needs for reparenting, to more positive and appropriate decisions we can make about ourselves, and to more helpful behavior.

---

[6] Jean Illsley Clarke, *Growing Up Again* (San Francisco: Harper & Row, 1989), p. 111.

It is important to remember that growing is a developmental process, and it occurs throughout life. Children often get impatient. They want to be grown up "right now," but they cannot—and neither can we. We need to be patient with ourselves. We may make some quick and immediate gains when we first begin reparenting. Then the process of consolidating and coordinating our new beliefs, attitudes, and behaviors may stretch out for an extended period. We may fall back at times. Growth is a process, a process of going along on a plateau, then falling back, then thrusting forward to a new level of maturity—reaching a plateau beyond where we had been before. This is the natural process and rhythm of growth. Both healing and growth need to be nurtured and encouraged, but neither can be hurried.

Even if our parents are dead, we may find it difficult to admit that we were abused or neglected as children. The need to defend our parents is so strong, says Alice Miller, a Swiss psychotherapist, that refusing to discuss or even acknowledge the abuse we received as children is the "Eleventh Commandment." It says, "Thou shalt not be aware." Miller's research has convinced her that because children are dependent on their parents for their very survival, both physically and emotionally, and because our society gives parents the message that they should do whatever is necessary to keep their kids in line, children are forced to suppress their experiences of abuse.

An extreme example of this recently surfaced in the city where I live. A young mother brought charges against her father for having raped and murdered her best friend when the two girls were quite young. Her memory of that event, which she had witnessed, along with many instances of sexual abuse she herself received from her father, had been so deeply buried that they did not begin to surface until her own daughter reached the age she had been at the time of the murder. With the help of a therapist, the mother was able to pull those wretchedly horrible memories out of her subconscious. After her memories were substantiated by other evidence, a jury found her father guilty of murder.

Most of us do not have such heinous childhood experiences buried within us, but most of us do have shame and pain and humiliation and abuse. We cannot deal effectively with our lives in the present until we have come to terms with these tormenting wounds from the past. Only as we are able to deal with these sensitive points within ourselves do we become effective in giving the respect and support needed by our own children and other people in our lives.

People often say, "But that's all in the past. Why not just leave it there? It was painful enough the first time. Why go through it again?" The answer is that unless we go back and deal with those wounds out of the past, we will continue to experience their pains over and over again. The old behaviors and the old patterns continue to haunt us in the present unless we find the insight and the courage to deal with them— to go through the reparenting process.

Reparenting is important but not easy. It is important enough to look more carefully at why it isn't easy. Besides the psychological allegiance we all feel to our parents, as reflected in Miller's work, a good many of us were reared in settings where unquestioning loyalty to parents was seen as a God-given responsibility. Before we ever got to Miller's Eleventh Commandment, many of us were well indoctrinated with the commandments Moses brought down from his encounter with God on Mount Sinai, including "Honor your father and your mother, that your days may be long in the land which the Lord your God gives you" (Exodus 20:12).

Most Old Testament scholars agree that "honoring" one's father and mother in ancient Israel meant caring for them in their old age, not giving total assent to all their perspectives and convictions. Even so, we still feel a paradoxical tension between being appropriately grateful to our parents for their love and care, respecting the wisdom of their experiences, and being faithful to our own insights and understandings. How much are we to submit to those in positions of authority and how much are we to trust our own experiences, insights, understandings, and convictions? We need to acknowledge and grapple with this complex dilemma.

In a speech I heard years ago from John Bradshaw, he suggested an image that has been helpful to me in getting at suppressed experiences of shame, humiliation, and abuse. Suppose I am learning to use a bow and arrow, and that I aim my arrow at a target. But suppose that, quite unintentionally, when I let the arrow fly from my bow, I miss the target, and my arrow goes through your shoulder. If you were to say, "That's OK. It doesn't matter. I know you didn't mean to do it. You were doing the very best you could," you would be both accurate in your assessment of my intentions and magnificent in your graciousness—but you would also be setting yourself up for a life of suppression and distortion and pain.

You have been wounded. If you refuse to acknowledge youan arrow sticking in your shoulder. Your whole life will become a giant accommodation as you develop new ways of reaching and holding and flexing your arm to compensate for the severe limitations imposed by your wound. There'll be many activities in which you simply cannot participate because your wound has left you crippled. And if the arrow in your shoulder goes unrecognized and untreated long enough, the poison from it will spread through your entire system, bringing sickness and an early death.

Many people have told me that this analogy has helped them come to terms with their woundedness, allowing them to acknowledge and take responsibility for serious injuries in their emotional structure. Acknowledgment allows us to quit being passive victims and to become accountable adults, living in reality and making the tough decisions necessary to deal appropriately with our wounds and to get on with our lives.

This brings us to the second part of our answer to "Where does self-esteem come from?" What we experienced in our families as we grew up provided the basis for our first decision about ourselves—about our capabilities and our worth, our self-esteem. Because it was a decision, it can be changed. And it needs to be changed to reflect the reality of who we are as adults in the world of today. *So now, as adults, regardless of our past histories, each of us has full, personal responsibility for our own self-esteem.*

Virginia Satir, the same therapist who wrote about all of us learning our self-esteem in the family in which we were reared, was equally emphatic in her assessment of this second part of the issue. I often heard her say, "Tell the people that regardless of what their backgrounds have been, their self-esteem can be raised. They can do it."

We made our first self-esteem decision in early childhood, at a precognitive stage, before we knew what we were doing. We made that value judgment about ourselves on the basis of the information and experiences available to us at the time. If we decided we were weak and dependent and powerless and wrong, that was probably a pretty reasonable decision, given the data we had at that time. The tragedy is that most of us go through the rest of our lives without making a new decision about ourselves. So the reality in the world outside us as adults doesn't fit with the realities going on inside.

As adults we have strengths, capabilities in independent living, the ability to affect our environment in significant ways, and experiences that have given us good insights and ideas. But if the last decision we made about ourselves was that we are weak, dependent, powerless, and wrong, we keep functioning out of that old decision. This doesn't work. The old decision is no longer accurate. It doesn't fit. This discrepancy means our lives keep getting messed up, which seems to confirm that we just don't have it.

I've been working with a young woman who has gone through her entire life believing herself to be mentally slow, academically inferior. Going to school was a real pain for her. She hated it. Yet, somewhere along the way, she became a compulsive reader. As I have come to know her, I experience her as unusually bright and insightful. Other people experience her that way also, but she has trouble accepting that new image of herself. Indeed, she seems to use her cleverness to invent reasons for proving that it is not so. She wants to think of herself as bright and insightful, but that image conflicts with how she's thought of herself all these years, which makes it exceedingly difficult for her to accept. So she has continued to stay stuck with her old, inappropriate, and inaccurate self-image—one that causes pain and distortion in her life as an adult. Except now she's beginning to change. She's made a courageous decision to go back to school.

To some extent or another, all of us live with old decisions that play havoc with our lives, distorting our behavior and every word we speak, our way of being in relationships, our hopes and dreams for the future. Continuing to cling to old decisions is the same as allowing our lives to be bound by the chains of fear—the fear that we're not enough, that who we are doesn't matter. Outer successes, no matter how spectacular, cannot change that self-image that we've carried as a part of who we are since early childhood.

The futility of attempting to find an authentic sense of worth on the basis of our achievements and public reputations is given classic illustration in one of the most familiar of Jesus' parables, the one about the publican and the Pharisee (Luke 18:9–14). Luke lets us know in the very first line that this parable was intended for those people who "trusted in themselves that they were righteous and despised others," in other words, people who had forgotten (if they ever knew) that "we're all in this thing together."

Jesus describes the Pharisee as one who "prayed thus with himself." Indeed, the Pharisee's prayer seems more like narcissistic self-talk than a prayer directed to God. His words amount to a recitation of what he sees to be his many commendable qualities, all headed by the statement, "I thank thee that I am not like other men . . . ." The Pharisee has no sense at all that "we're all in this thing together." He uses the structures and rituals of his religion to construct an image of himself as separate and superior, an image that he is committed to maintaining even though it is inaccurate and viciously destructive to his relationships with other people. The publican, by contrast, was not even able to lift his eyes to God. In his despair over his obvious failures and shortcomings, he smote his breast and cried, "God, be merciful to me, a sinner."

Jesus concludes the parable by saying of the publican, "I tell you, this man went down to his house justified rather than the other." Jesus did not say that the publican was blameless of the sins that weighed so heavily on him, or even that he was better than the Pharisee. What he said about the publican was that whatever stood between this man and his God, between this man and his own deepest self, had been removed. He no longer had to try to "make up" for anything. He didn't have to play games with himself to try to make it appear that he was good. He was justified. He was right with God and right with himself. He was able to move on, to grow.

His willingness to look honestly at himself and his life is a marvelous example of an authentic faith in one's own personal worth. The publican was able to acknowledge and accept the reality of the destructive evil in his life. Acknowledging that he needed help and asking for it, his confession put him in a position to do something positive in the direction of changing.

In contrast to the Pharisee, the publican saw himself as he was—as part of the whole of wounded humanity.

This is where we benefit by taking responsibility for our own lives, for two reasons. The first is that nothing can be done to raise our self-esteem unless we acknowledge that it is a problem, just as alcoholics can do nothing about their condition until they've acknowledged and accepted it as existing. The second reason is that no one else can give us healthy self-esteem. We made the first decision. We are the only ones who can make the new, corrective one.

The very act of taking responsibility for our own self-esteem expresses growing self-esteem. People with low self-esteem tell themselves things such as: "Much as I would like to, I'm just not strong enough to be more decisive. I wasn't raised that way, and my husband [or wife] would kill me if I tried. If I were brighter or healthier or more outgoing or a better speaker or able to think on my feet or more hardnosed and less sensitive to other people's feelings, then I could stand up for myself better. But as it is, I can't." Messages such as these represent both low self-esteem and the negative self-talk that keeps us chained within it.

One of the best ways to check our level of self-esteem is by paying attention to how much we engage in "victim talk," that is, habitual patterns of speech or thought in which we depict ourselves as helpless victims of persons and conditions outside of us. Our words provide a marvelous mirror as to what we really think of ourselves, and our negative self-images have a way of becoming self-fulfilling prophesies. "I just can't get to work on time. It's a wonder I got here at all this morning. With all the maniacs out there on the streets, I'm lucky to be alive. If this company promoted people on the basis of hard work rather than who you know, I could get the position I deserve." By using victim talk, we disempower ourselves. We confine ourselves in images of helplessness.

Closely related to victim talk is "negative self-talk."
Jack Canfield, one of the best-known U.S. speakers on self-
esteem, reports that most of us say something to ourselves
about ourselves 50,000 times a day; on average, 40,000 of
those messages are negative. This is not only a signal of our
low self-esteem, it is another way in which we lock ourselves
into that old, crippling, precognitive decision.

So, if I decided as an infant that I was weak, unwanted,
and unworthy, then 40,000 times a day I may say something to
myself like, "There you go again! You're always goofing up.
You never will get it right. Everyone knows you're a big
dummy and you are! No wonder you have so few friends and
so little respect at work." I'm not likely to move very far from
that long-ago decision. I can spend my entire life making
excuses.

One step in taking responsibility for our own self-esteem
is to recognize when we're talking like victims or giving ourselves negative messages. Once we understand such behavior
as an indication that we're still operating out of an old childhood decision—out of the conviction that "I'm not enough"—
we can reexmine the evidence and make new decisions. People
with healthy self-esteem have problems, difficulties, and
hardships; but they don't respond by blaming those conditions on someone else or condemning themselves for mistakes. Recently published studies show that such people
achieve more, have more satisfying lives, and have fewer
physical sicknesses. They take responsibility for their own
lives. They choose to see themselves as capable human beings, and they take whatever steps seem appropriate to move
on with their growth as persons.

Self-esteem is a decision we make about ourselves, a
value judgment about whether we see ourselves as lovable
and capable human beings. To our frequent amazement and
despair, that decision has nothing to do with anything outside, how we look or how successful we are. When we gain that

honor, that position, that relationship, that level of income which we were sure would give us the confidence and sense of worth for which we had always yearned, we find that it has not. Our long-standing view of ourselves has not changed. We need both a new image of (new beliefs) about ourselves *and* experiences of ourselves functioning successfully out of that new image. We not only need a new self-image as persons capable of functioning in the world in a new way; we need to do it: to act on our new self-image.

For example, if I have never trusted myself to be honest, then I face two aspects of change. Besides daring to believe that I am capable of being honest and picturing myself in that new image, I must also choose to act in ways that express that new understanding of myself. No matter how much some dear friend or trusted counselor may tell me I am capable of being honest with myself and others, my new sense of self will not become a part of me until I choose to change in both these respects. First I need to believe I am capable of honesty. Second, I need to act on that new faith by behaving as an honest person.

Similarly, it's impossible for me to give healthy self-esteem to someone else. Indeed, it may be counterproductive to attempt to do so. If my friend is convinced she's incapable of love, she may interpret my insistence that she is as my refusal to take her seriously. She may think I am discounting her deepest personal reality, or that I am trying to take over her life. Either reaction would be at least partially true. My paternalistic treatment would indeed indicate I do not regard her as having an adequate understanding.

All of us can, however, be helpful to others as they work toward higher self-esteem. We do this by treating them with dignity and respect. In the illustration just cited, I could say to my friend, "I understand that you don't feel capable of loving, and I'm sorry. And even though I know this is how you feel, I'm not convinced that it's an accurate final judgment about who you are. You are important enough to me that I would be willing to spend some time talking with you about it if you care to do so, or to help you find someone with more skill than I have to talk with you. Not feeling capable of love was horribly painful for me. I've found that for me it all circled around not feeling I was loved."

As Ian Macpherson, the Scottish pastor, used to say, "Be kind. Everyone you meet is fighting a hard battle." We're all in this thing together, and we can help others by identifying with their struggles. Otherwise, we may fall into the tragic assumption that we, our families, and those who agree with us are closer to the truth or closer to God than those who are different. Forgetting that we are all in this thing together not only cuts us off from a nurturing kind of contact with others, it also cuts us off from our own humanity.

Jesus performed his acts of healing by being with people in their pain. Throughout his entire ministry, he walked among and talked to people who were ill and unacceptable to the rest of society. He dared to touch the open sores and the rotting flesh of lepers, who were forbidden by law to come within ten feet of nonlepers. Healing happens as we acknowledge our oneness with all humanity, as we are willing to feel their pains and our own.

This recognition that we are all in this thing together is what I find to be the positive aspect of the doctrine of original sin. Another side of it strikes me as monstrously destructive. The church's emphasis on the doctrine of original sin has often hidden and even destroyed a much more important and more securely founded scriptural teaching. It is what the Roman Catholic priest/teacher/writer Matthew Fox calls the doctrine of original blessing.

> Original blessing is prior to any sin, original or less than original . . .. The time has come to let anthropocentric go, and with it to let the preoccupation

with human sinfulness give way to attention to divine grace.[7]

From the very first page, the Bible says God looked at his creation and "it was very good!" In what is probably the best known verse in the New Testament, we are assured that "God so loved the world that he gave . . ." (John 3:16). The Bible's continuing narrative seems to me to be the story of a God of unconditional love who refuses to give up on his people. Human beings are worth God's gift of himself. Surely Fox is correct in asking us to consider paying more attention to this dominant, positive theme.

The traditional scriptural foundation for the doctrine of original sin is found in the second of the two creation stories in the book of Genesis, in Adam and Eve's disobedience to God's command and in their consequent expulsion from the Garden of Eden (Genesis 3:1–24). Yet Jewish scholars, who have been reading and interpreting those verses for a thousand years longer than Christian theologians, do not find a doctrine of original sin within them. Matthew Fox reports that the twentieth-century Jewish prophet Elie Wiesel says specifically that "The concept of original sin is alien to Jewish tradition."

Nor does Christian literature mention original sin until Augustine propounded it in the fifth century. Fox's careful research indicates that the idea began to appear in Augustine's later writings, that it grew out of his preoccupation with his own sinfulness as described in his "Confessions," and that it is based on a mistranslation of the Bible.

What is instructive to me is that this doctrine, with the shakiest of scriptural support, obviously caught on and

---

[7] Matthew Fox, *Original Blessing* (Santa Fe, NM: Bear & Company, 1983), p. 26.

prospered. It is now a part of the theological structure of virtually every branch of the Christian tradition. This suggests something important about human fearfulness: that we may be all too willing to accept negative judgments about ourselves. Maybe low self-esteem set us up to accept a deprecating verdict about our human character, a verdict that has now become a self-fulfilling prophesy. We pass it on from preachers to parents to children, generation after generation.

Many years ago, as a young pastor, I read an article asserting that anyone who does not believe in the doctrine of original sin has never been around young children. The writer explained that young children are very self-centered. Their whole view of the world pivots around their personal sense of comfort. If a baby is resting comfortably in mother's arms with a full stomach and a dry diaper, the world is fine, no matter what may be amiss with anyone else anywhere else. On the other hand, the world and the baby's family may be in a state of harmony and peace, but if the baby's personal circumstances are uncomfortable, the baby is miserable. Such an absolute focus on oneself was a clear indication that we have a sinful preoccupation with ourselves from birth.

As a young father, I immediately agreed with the writer's line of reasoning. I had personal experiences of how a baby's needs, no matter how minor they may have appeared to me, could completely disrupt my work schedule or recreational plans. That kind of insensitive, demanding selfishness was surely indisputable evidence that we human beings come into this world immersed in a sinful preoccupation with our own personal comfort.

Nowadays I totally disagree. I think this is a ridiculously misinformed example, even though as a pastor I often used it to illustrate the doctrine of original sin. Now I'm convinced that every child has a God-given right to tons of personal attention and to the assurance that he or she is prized, wanted, welcome, loved, adored—even if the communication of that assurance poses a major disruption to the family's schedule. Our responsibility as parents is to use every means available to us to show our kids that they are precisely as Jesus regarded all human beings to be: of unconditional and incomparable worth.

This is not meant to condone the behavior of adults who act like spoiled children. Adults who demand that their needs be met without regard for anyone else are people who didn't experience their dignity and worth as children. Though they may not even be aware of it themselves, those adults are full of a painful outrage because their rightful legacy was denied them. As a result, their lives are controlled by the fear that they do not matter. This fear may express itself either in a self-effacing withdrawal from the world and life, or in behavior that is angry, manipulative, and destructive.

Ray Gott, a captain in the Los Angeles County Sheriff's Department who was also a member of the California Self-Esteem Task Force, told me repeatedly that we are daily losing our battle with the gangs in that city. On the basis of a lifelong career in law enforcement, and after heading the sheriff's work with gangs for more than two years, Gott is convinced that only when we do some "front-end work," that is, allow these young people to develop new and more affirming convictions about themselves and their possibilities, will we have any hope of stemming the destruction.

Whether in gangs or in government or grain fields or suburban gardens or giant skyscrappers, adults who are still functioning out of inadequate and inaccurate images of themselves from childhood now have a chance, and a major responsibility: to relearn about their worth and dignity. Whatever our views about original sin, most of us can probably accept the reality that we are sinners: that is, we've not attained the fullness of the humanity for which we were created and for which we yearn within ourselves. We do hateful and destructive things, not only to our so-called enemies but also to those whom we love and to ourselves. Evil exists. Hateful and destructive deeds happen. Let's accept and be very clear about our need for forgiveness.

Then let us move on. Being sinners is not the last or definitive word on us. If the Christian gospel says anything, it is that we are free to rejoice in the faith that the God who created us in love, and in his own image, loves us still—that he has acted to forgive and accept us, unconditionally. Recognizing our sinfulness is to recognize that this is not the condition for which we were created, nor is it what God sees when he looks at us. We are loved. We can rejoice in the wonder of being so massively precious and prized and loved. And then let us become instruments by which that forgiveness and acceptance and love are communicated to others, especially our kids.

The single most definitive study I've seen on the possibilities for communicating high affirmation, with a consequent impact on helping children to learn healthy self-esteem, was a joint project carried on by Syracuse University (New York) and Far West Laboratory (San Francisco). In what they called "Long Range Impact of An Early Intervention with Low-Income Children and Their Families," researchers went into a low-income neighborhood in Syracuse in the early 1970s and recruited 108 women in the last trimester of pregnancy. Home visitors were trained to make weekly visits with the mothers and other family members. During the course of the five years of the project, these visitors brought all kinds of helpful information to the families; but their single biggest task was to be a personal friend: "to act in support of rather than as substitutes for parents . . . ."[8] A second main focus of the program was to provide consistently positive day care for

---

[8] "Long-Range Impact of An Early Intervention with Low-Income Children and Their Families" (San Francisco: Far West Laboratory, 1987), p. 2.

the children. This was done for 50 weeks a year for the first five years of the lives of the children in the program.

Workers operated within the assumptions that the children were capable of learning, understanding that their actions and choices affected others, cooperating with and showing concern for the others, and expressing their creativity, excitement, curiosity and individuality more fully.

> Additionally, these children were treated as special creations, each with particular skills and specialties that would be appreciated by and useful to the larger society; these special powers were protected and allowed to rise to ascendance by the adults who spent the daytime hours with them. [9]

After the five years, the researchers left. They came back ten years later to find out what had happened. The results were truly amazing. "Only 6% of the program children in the follow-up sample as compared to 22% of the control children have been processed as probation cases by the County Probation Department."

Encourage and support the parents. Encourage and support the children. Believe in them, in their worth and capability. Encourage them to believe in themselves. The results could hardly be more convincing. The number of children from the project group who had gotten into trouble with the law was one-fourth that of their peers in the control group. Even more amazing, the severity of the trouble the project group got into represented *one-tenth* the cost to law enforcement agencies. In short, the children who were given conscious encouragement and support, treated as "special creations," turned out to be *ten times* more likely to lead personally and socially responsible lives.

---

[9] Ibid, p. 2.

This happened in an inner city ghetto among low-income, largely minority young people—precisely where gangs and drugs so often rule the day. Besides the obvious practical conclusions to be drawn from this study, the philosophical implications are equally important. What is the true nature of being human? What is the most helpful and effective way to nurture human beings to useful maturity?

How do people learn to be effective, fulfilled, and responsible human beings? A book of profound insight that explores the deep mysteries of being human is *The Denial of Death* by Ernest Becker; it won the 1974 Pulitzer Prize for Literature. Born and educated within the Jewish tradition, Becker claims no personal faith commitment in this book (if he does so elsewhere I am not aware of it); yet, drawing on his vast command of acknowledged giants in both philosophy and psychology, he presents the most convincing case for the depth and integrity and practicability of the Christian faith that I have ever read.

He attempts to explain what he says none of us dare face in the fullness of its terrifying reality: the impossible contradiction of the human condition.

> Man is literally split in two: he has an awareness of his own splendid uniqueness in that he sticks out of nature with a towering majesty, and yet he goes back into the ground a few feet in order blindly and dumbly to rot and disappear forever. It is a terrifying dilemma to be in and to have to live with.[10]

The "terrifying dilemma" is that we human beings experience ourselves, on the one hand, as a little lower than the angels—able to be moved to the depths of our beings by a magnificent sunset, by a Bach oratorio, by the mysterious

---

[10] From *The Denial of Death* by Ernest Becker. Copyright © 1973 by The Free Press, a Division of Macmillan, Inc. Reprinted by permission of the publisher.

wonder of life in a small child, by the marvels of quantum physics—and, on the other hand, if hit by a speeding automobile, to be as splattered and dead and unmoving and powerless as a grasshopper. Human beings must therefore find some basis for believing that, in spite of this inescapable contradiction, we are of worth, our being does have some significance after all, the pains and struggles and disappointments we experience are somehow in some lasting way worth it, and that who we are and what we think and do does make some essential difference. We are all engaged in this effort.

> What I have tried to do is . . . to suggest that the problem of heroics is the central one of human life, that it goes deeper into human nature than anything else because it is based on organismic narcissism and on the child's need for self-esteem as the condition for his life.[11]

We don't want self-esteem to matter so much. We would prefer our success or failure as human beings to rest on some other, more manageable basis. But from a vast spectrum of sources—medical, psychological, sociological, philosophical, theological, and everyday life experiences—there emerges a solid and consistent foundation for asserting that the essential human quest is to find and acquire and be nurtured by a satisfying and sustaining sense of self-esteem.

From every conceivable angle, this chapter cites evidence that our early years are crucial in developing a positive sense of worth. In turn, the child's self-esteem provides the best possible foundation for a productive and satisfying life as an adult. Rather than disparaging or discouraging our fellow human beings, we best serve persons and society by prizing, valuing, encouraging, supporting, and affirming each other. The other side of this is that, regardless of what our background may be, each adult is totally and personally re-

---

[11] Ibid, p. 7.

sponsible for his or her own self-esteem. Whatever our
present level of self-esteem, we can raise it. And if we are to
raise it, then each of us, personally, must be the one who
achieves high self-esteem by choosing to affirm for ourselves
the assurance expressed so pointedly by Bernie Siegel: "You
are not that unloved child any more."

CHAPTER FOUR

"To Choose One's Own Way"

As we have seen, other people, especially our parents, occupy a place of fundamental importance in the development of our self-esteem. Our sense of ourselves has its initial basis in how the psychologically important people in our lives teach us to think and feel about ourselves. That's a given. The tragedy occurs if we never get beyond that: if we live our lives at the mercy of how others may, at any given moment, choose to feel about us. This underlies one of the foundational statements to come out of the self-esteem movement: *We are not in this world to live up to anyone else's expectations.*

Our lives are often twisted and distorted when we make choices as if our worth and success as human beings depended on our living up to the very particular and personal expectations of the people who nurtured our growth. When we base our sense of ourselves on the judgment of others, we give up our integrity and allow our lives to become something less than fully human. We become the victims of the whims and purposes of the people around us.

So, even though the judgments of other people are an inevitable and sometimes necessary part of our sense of worth, we alone are finally responsible for our own self-esteem. If we find ourselves unwilling or unable to accept that responsibility, that in itself may be a glaring red warning light that we suffer from low self-esteem. Furthermore, the refusal or unwillingness to take responsibility for our own self-esteem is also a highly reliable indicator that we're likely to stay stuck with that low self-esteem.

Most of us have come honestly to our painful and destructive condition of low self-esteem. Because human infants are so totally dependent on their parents for their very survival, all of us are mightily influenced by what our parents expected or demanded of us. In that highly vulnerable and dependent condition, it was reasonable to believe that "good" is what our parents called good, and "bad" is what they called bad. As children we believe we are good when we do things that please our parents and bad when we displease them. Children see their parents as infallible, which is why early family influences are so incredibly important, and why we tend to see the world and ourselves through the filter of these highly subjective notions of goodness and badness all our lives.

Here's a somewhat extreme but dramatically illustrative example. It comes from Reuel Howe, an Episcopalian priest and the author of one of the most widely read and discussed books in the churches during the 1950s, *Man's Need and God's Action*. Howe wrote of a young mother who became pregnant for the second time and shortly thereafter fell into a deep depression. She eventually became catatonic, making it impossible for the doctors to get at the source of her illness. When a therapist was able to hypnotize her, however, the patient related a recurring dream. In it she was attempting to scale an icy mountain. Her mother and grandmother stood at the summit, looking down at her. The young woman's efforts to climb the mountain were futile. For every step forward, she would slide back two, symbolizing her frustration and failure.

Finally, through the therapist's patience and skill, the young woman could talk about the dream in a conscious state. It turned out that she had grown up believing that her mother expected her to have a career on the stage as a dancer and that her grandmother expected her to be sexually pure. Even though she had a loving and attentive husband, when she became pregnant for the second time it was clear to the young mother's subconscious that she was not going to fulfill either of those expectations. She could not climb the mountain her family had set before her. So, rather than deal with this massive sense of failure, she died emotionally. She withdrew from the land of the living.

Howe used that story to distinguish real guilt from neurotic guilt. Real guilt springs from the failure to be the human beings God created us to be. This can be forgiven. Neurotic guilt is more difficult. It is what we feel when we fail to live up to what we believe to be the expectations of those people whose affirmations and acceptance are important to us. It is not a failure before God or the moral order of the universe. Neurotic guilt is not real guilt; nothing exists to be forgiven. So forgiveness has no impact on neurotic guilt.

The only solution to the pain and distortions of neurotic guilt is to change the self-expectations from which it arises. We need to identify any unrealistic and misguided expectations we have of ourselves and then examine their sources and their appropriateness. As needed, we can replace them with expectations that are more realistic and of our own choosing. The young woman in the story, for example, worked through her psychological past and decided it was fine with God for her to be a wife and mother. When she was free from the pressure of other people's expectations, she recovered her health and her ability to function effectively as a wife, mother, and human being.

The particular homes, churches, schools, and communities in which we learn our faith give us a particular emphasis and set of priorities that become, for us, virtually indistinguishable from the essential tenets of that faith itself. For example, many who grew up surrounded by the constant reminder that it is "better to give than to receive" interpreted that to mean they were good and acceptable people only when they were giving. It was a sign of weakness or even failure to receive. Yet, it is as much a spiritual reality as a psychological one that the only people who *can* give are those who have received. Individuals with psychological barriers against receiving tend to become barren and bitter. Generally speaking, they have difficulty entering into satisfying and vulnerable relationships with others. Their ability to participate in and maintain wholesome and healthy interchange with others is significantly jeapordized when they use religious convictions to support their resistance to receiving.

So what are our options? If we say we're not going to teach our children any religious faith, allowing them to make up their minds for themselves, we are, in effect, teaching them that we have no spiritual convictions worth sharing. At the other end of the continuum, we may present a set of doctrines as being absolutely infallible and essential and, in that rigidity, deny our own fallibility and our children's opportunity to learn to take responsibility for themselves and their lives.

Each point along the spectrum between these two extremes has its own tradeoffs. My own reflections have brought me to believe that valuing our own worth and wanting to share the benefits of our own experiences need to be balanced with an appreciation for the dignity, worth, and choice-making responsibilities of our kids. In loyalty to ourselves, we can share what is most meaningful and important to us. In loyalty to our children, we can encourage them to be in touch with and to trust their own experiences, intuitions, and integrity.

Paul Tournier, a Swiss psychiatrist, was a deeply committed (and conservative) Christian who wrote extensively and effectively to a world-wide audience in the 1960s and '70s. One of his thoughts was that it is a mistake for Christians to expect a young child to commit his or her life to Christ before being old enough to understand that he or she has a life to commit. In other words, asking for a life commitment from children is usually a manipulation on the part of and for the sake of the parents and church leaders—with destructive consequences for the children. Extracting a life commitment from children actually prevents them from getting in touch with their real selves and respecting their own choice-making responsibilities.

This is a part of the background that has convinced me that we are not in this world to live up to anyone else's expectations. What's more, *I claim Jesus as one of my strongest supporters for this conviction.* I find strong evidence for this in a well-known but terribly confusing quote from Jesus: "You, therefore, must be perfect, as your heavenly Father is perfect" (Matthew 5:48).

Exactly what Jesus said turns out to be very different from what most of us have always assumed that he said. Most English translations of the Bible use *perfect* to translate the Greek work *teleios*. This word is more accurately translated in today's vernacular as *whole* or *complete*. That simple understanding completely changes the context of our thinking. It's one thing to believe that Jesus commands us to be whole or complete, and quite another to believe that our God-given obligation is to be perfect, with all the personal, neurotic expectations we bring to that word.

Furthermore, when we read that sentence in context and not as an isolated thought, we discover that Jesus has told us precisely what he means by wholeness. In the previous part of the paragraph, he defines the wholeness of God: "for he makes his sun rise on the evil and on the good, and sends rain on the just and the unjust." (Matthew 5:45b). In other words, the wholeness of God is that he acts out of the integrity of who he is. He behaves in ways that are consistent with his own deepest self, regardless of what people do or do not do to him.

Lest someone think I am using a liberal, psychological perspective to distort the original meaning of this passage, let me quote from the writings of the Scottish cleric Dr. William Barclay, one of the most respected and conservative biblical scholars of this century.

> So, then, a man will be *teleios* if he fulfills the purpose for which he was created. For what purpose was man created? The Bible leaves us in no doubt as to that . . . *Man was created to be like God.* The characteristic of God is this universal benevolence, this unconquerable good will, this constant seeking of the highest good of every man. The great characteristic of God is to love saint and sinner alike. No matter what men do to him, God seeks nothing but their highest good.[1]

This illustrates that accurate information about scriptural translations and meanings often gives us a whole new understanding of the texture and direction of what we read in the Bible. In this command, for example, instead of being compelled to be perfect—which in the minds and imaginations of a good many of us has always meant not smoking, not drinking, not swearing, not thinking any angry or impure thoughts, not doing any angry or impure deeds—we are called to be whole. Being whole means loving as God loves, acting

---

[1] William Barclay, *The Gospel of Matthew, Vol. 1* (Philadelphia: Westminster Press, 1975), p. 178.

out of our own integrity, dealing with people on the basis of who we are and what we are in ourselves. It does not mean making choices according to what other people may or may not do to us or say to us. We are to act out of an awareness of our own worthiness and that of all human beings. We are to treat people in a way that is consistent with who we are, without any regard at all to how deserving they are, who they are, or what they have done to us.

The significance of this stretches far beyond theological theory. It touches the deepest and most personal fabric of human life. For example, I am always saddened by accounts of the families of victims of some hellacious crime who demand that the last ounce of revenge be inflicted on the perpetrators. These grieving people seem to believe that their sorrow will be lessened if those who brutalized their love ones are dealt with in an equally severe and brutal manner. It is not difficult to understand the intensity of their pain. But when we refuse to be compassionate and humane to others, regardless of who they are or what they have done, we are left without those essential human qualities in ourselves. In addition, our vindictiveness only adds to the world's already overwhelming need for mercy, compassion, and understanding. By the same token, my life is enriched when I hear of families in similar circumstances who overcome their pain and bitterness by extending care and understanding to the very people who have been the source of their grief. Even as I write these words, there is a magnificent example in this morning's newspaper: Terry Anderson's words of compassion for his Arab captors after 2,455 days as a hostage, much of it in solitary confinement.

For years I've had hanging on my wall a quote from the award-winning author from South Africa, Alan Paton: "Life has taught me, and this is my luck, that active loving saves one from a morbid preoccupation with the shortcomings of society and the waywardness of men." This is another way of describing the difference between self-esteem and other-esteem.

The biblical passage described earlier tells us to think and act out of our own integrity, out of love and compassion, rather than becoming captive to the thoughts or actions or words of the people around us. No matter who those people may happen to be, we are not in this world to live up to their expectations.

Other faiths also express this philosophy. An ancient rabbinical story does so with dramatic poignancy.

> The chassidic saint Rav Zussye of Tarnifal trembled before his death: I am about to face the Holy One, blessed be He, and justify my sojourn in the world. If He will ask me: Zussye, why were you not like Moses? I shall respond, because you did not grant me the powers you granted Moses. If He will ask me: Zussye, why were you not like Rabbi Akiba? I shall respond, because you did not grant me the powers you granted Rabbi Akiba. But the Almighty will not ask me why I was not like Moses, or why I was not like Rabbi Akiba. The Almighty will ask me: Zussye, why were you not like Zussye, why did you not fulfill the potential which was Zussye, and it is for this question that I tremble.[2]

Something within the rabbinic tradition apparently understands this truth clearly. The renowned rabbi, teacher, and philosopher Martin Buber, author of the "I–Thou" concept, wrote:

> Every man's foremost task is the actualization of his unique, unprecedented and never recurring potentialities, and not the repetition of something that another, and be it even the greatest, has already achieved.[3]

---

[2] Dov Peretz Elkins, Ed., *Glad To Be Me* (Rochester, NY: Growth Associates, 1989), p. 49.
[3] Ibid, p. 71.

The spiritual basis for assuming that we are not in this world to live up to anyone else's expectations has solid and saintly spiritual support. We need to be our own authentic selves, to find our own way. Doing so is not a simple or solitary task. Ironically, we cannot do it all by ourselves, independently from the nurturing support of others.

In their own insecurities, our parents wanted us to be pleasing to the world, at least to that portion of the world that was important to them. So, usually without being aware of what they were doing, even sometimes vigorously denying that they were doing it, our parents taught us that it's imperative to please the world. Furthermore, even if unwittingly, they taught us what we need to do to please the world. As if we needed still another burden, almost all parents in our society teach their children what their parents taught them: that it is necessary to conform and to distort their personalities to meet the expectations of important, worth-giving people.

In actual fact, the important people in the world of adolescents are their peers. Whether we find the group that suits our tastes or acquire tastes that conform to the group we want to join is an open question. It's probably some of both. Meanwhile, the very parents who object so strenuously to their children's conformity to dominant teenage standards in dress and music and behavior are often the same parents who worked so hard to teach their kids the importance of being liked. They wanted their kids to conform to the parents' interests, but it seldom works that way.

The domination and destructiveness of today's gangs have become a common and frightening phenomenon, especially in the inner city but now showing up almost everywhere. Many students of gang psychology have noted that members give each other precisely what they needed but did not get from their families: acceptance, attention, encouragement, and a sense of being needed and of belonging. The cost, of course, is the loss of freedom to make their own choices and to develop their talents in ways that are productive to them as well as to society.

Just as we needed the acceptance of our parents as children in order to become our own unique selves, peer acceptance is an essential part of our development in adolescence. For good or ill, and probably some of both, our identities are shaped by how our peer group responds to the self we present. We have all known of bright people who refused to study, conscientious workers who became derelicts, superb athletes who got hooked on drugs—all because of their need for acceptance by their peers. Even those of us who avoided such extreme reversals can be sure that our personalities were heavily imprinted by peer-group pressures.

The result is that most of us enter adulthood with the notion that what other people think and say about us is more accurate and far more important than what we think and feel about ourselves. Those who deny this most vigorously are, quite often, precisely the ones who believe it the most. Their desire for acceptance and approval haunts and controls them, which is why they feel so compelled to deny its existence.

As adults we belong to groups and find friends who support the image we have chosen, or to which we have acceded. Our enemies become those whose convictions or dress or behavior seem to threaten the treasures around which our identities are formed. Certain siblings fight all the time with each other, for instance, unless one of them is threatened by someone outside the family. Then they become a supportive unit against the outsider. This seems to support the notion that, for all their differences, these siblings find strength in their identity as members of the family and, therefore, they join together against any threat to that source of security and worth. A similar thing happens when nations are threatened by other nations. Even the most glaring differences are forgotten in the heat of standing together against a common enemy. We all have a basic need to belong, a need which, if not properly understood and handled, has the power to destroy our identities and integrities as individual persons.

Because of the universality and intensity of this need, what we all too often assume is our self-esteem is really other-esteem. We say we don't care what other people think of us, but we conform nevertheless. One of the most tragic but seldom recognized consequences of accepting other people's judgments of us is that in doing so we allow those other people to be in charge of our lives. When we allow them to decide about our worth, they also control our thinking, behavior, relationships, and ambitions. This is a painful, damnable condition; yet we cannot even begin to deal with it—let alone change it—until we are willing to acknowledge it. We need to recognize that we have allowed other people to form our opinions about whether we are good or bad, worthwhile or useless.

To understand how this process works, we can turn to one of the first books by the noted psychologist Rollo May:

> The authoritarian shackling which the person endures earliest in life is external: the growing infant, whether a child of exploitative parents or, let us say, a Jew born in a country with anti-Semitic prejudice, is the victim of the external circumstances. The child must face and adjust to, by hook or crook, the world he is born into. But gradually in anyone's development the authoritarian problems become *internalized:* the growing person takes over the rules and plants them in himself; and he tends to act all his life through as though he still were fighting the original forces which would enslave him. But now it has become an *internal* conflict. Fortunately, there is a happy moral in this point: since the person has taken over the suppressive forces and keeps them going in himself, he has also in himself the power to get over them.

> For adults, then, who are engaged in rediscovering
> themselves, the battle is centrally an internal
> one. *The struggle to become a person takes place
> within the person himself* [emphasis added].[4]

In developing healthy self-esteem, it is absolutely essential to take back the authority we have given away, to
reclaim our right to decide for ourselves about ourselves. This
is true regardless of what our background has been. Our
struggle to become actualizing persons with healthy self-
esteem is not, finally, with our parents or anyone else. *It is
within us.*

Becoming free, grown-up, self-authenticating human
beings is not an easy job. It requires facing up to and setting
aside much of what we have used for the foundation and
structure of our lives from the very beginning. May uses the
insights of the ancient Greek story of Orestes, who killed his
mother, to explain this process of taking responsibility.

> Obviously, the moral of the Orestes drama is not
> that everyone get a gun and kill his mother. What
> has to be killed . . . is the infantile ties of depen-
> dency which bind the person to the parents, and
> thereby keep him from loving outwardly and cre-
> ating independently.[5]

The example of Orestes is both shocking and helpful. It
focuses attenion on the urgency and the personal responsibility involved in becoming our own parents, taking charge of
our own lives, and owning ourselves. To do so is an extremely
difficult and painful task—emotionally almost as unthinkable
as killing one's own parents. I take May's figurative imagery of
killing our parents to mean that we must come to the point
where our sense of ourselves is no longer controlled by the

---

[4] Rollo May, *Man's Search for Himself* (New York: W. W. Norton,
1953), p. 118.
[5] Ibid, p. 117.

approval or disapproval of our parents. At first this situation is difficult for most of us even to imagine. Yet, to gain access to our own judgments, which allows us to live our own lives as mature adults, we need to make choices that are independent of our parents' judgments about us.

If May's use of the word *kill* seems too harsh, remember that Jesus of Nazareth consistently spoke of dying in order to live. On one occasion (Matthew 10:34b–36), he even said his purpose in coming was to create conflict within families.

> I have not come to bring peace, but a sword. For I have come to set a man against his father, and a daughter against her mother, and a daughter-in-law against her mother-in-law; and a man's foes will be those of his own household.

While Jesus certainly did not come preaching hatred or erecting barriers, he recognized that people who did not grow up and become independent could not choose to receive love or to give it. We turn members of our households into enemies if we cling to them, if we allow their expectations to determine our lives. This includes the members of our households of faith—our churches. To think and decide for ourselves, we must move beyond being automatically compliant to the advice and opinions of even those we love the most. They may respond with outrage, perhaps even hatred.

Clinging compulsively to anything—people, ideas, beliefs, or habits—prevents us from becoming the authentic and unique human beings that Jesus says God created us to be. This is true even if we cling to something sacred and holy, such as a church, the Bible, religious rituals, or spiritual sayings. (Chapter 7 examines the role of the church as an essential nurturing community that allows us to grow by permitting us to stand up to the very people on whom we are dependent, in order to devlop a sense of our own individuality and uniqueness.) When Jesus called his first disciples to follow him, he promised them nothing and gave them nothing to which to cling—except that out there on the journey, going they knew not where, *he would be with them.*

It requires enormous effort to live in the world on our own, no longer clinging to our parents or institutions or ideas or achievements or a pleasing public reputation or anything else to keep us safe. Yet we cannot have healthy *self*-esteem if we do not make that enormously difficult, painful, and scary decision. We remain dependent children forever if our sense of power and worth depends on someone or something else.

So how do we kill our dependency on others? As is often the case with issues related to self-esteem, those qualities that are *characteristics* of healthy self-esteem are also the *conditions* necessary for achieving it. The courage to be one's self, to take full responsibility for one's own life, must be born out of a sense of being "enough," able to make it. In short, the courage to be one's self, which is an essential characteristic of healthy self-esteem, is also a prerequisite for achieving it. In fact, back in the 1950s, long before anyone was talking about self-esteem, May used that phrase in his description of the courage it takes to be an authentic person: "Courage arises from one's sense of dignity and self-esteem; and one is un-courageous because he thinks too poorly of himself."[6]

To think highly of ourselves we must have courage, and to be courageous we must think highly of ourselves. So where do we begin? In a sense, that is the question to which this entire book is addressed, a question to which we must necessarily return again and again, in our lives as well as in this book. But here's a clue. In his best-selling *Fire in the Belly*, Sam Keen advises: "Where you stumble and fall, there you will find your treasure."[7]

---

[6] Ibid, p. 200.
[7] Sam Keen, *Fire in the Belly* (New York: Bantam, 1991), p. 226.

My own life experiences, and those of others, lead me to believe that growth almost always happens as a result of a crisis: some event or experience that makes it inescapably clear that our old ways of seeing, thinking, behaving, understanding, and relating aren't working any more. Many times I have heard or said, "What seemed at the time like a total tragedy turned out to be the best thing that ever happened to me!" A crisis, and the honest recognition of it, are often, if not always, the occasion for new growth. The fall reveals the treasure.

Apparently we resist changing until circumstances force us to do so. Even then some people refuse to change. In the stress of a crisis, some people give up. They die spiritually and emotionally, if not physically. For others, crises become the occasion for a new life. They reach down into themselves and get in touch with depths they'd never imagined they had. They break past inner barriers that had confined them as prisoners. Examining and rejecting old, outworn, inadequate images and expectations, they choose new and more realistic appraisals. They hear, as if for the first time, the messages of new hope—from the gospel, from the heart, or from people such as the surgeon Bernie Siegel, who tells us: "You are not that unloved child anymore." This conviction, that we are truly loved, seems to be the essential basis for the courage necessary for positive change. That courage is required for responding positively to a crisis and turning it into an opportunity for growth.

Somewhere in his writings, Deitrich Bonhoeffer put forth the notion that a Christian never grows until he puts himself in a position where faith becomes a possibility. Most of us do everything we can to avoid that position, even those of us who talk a great deal about faith. In actuality we work very hard to create a world of such absolute certainty and security that we never have to rely on faith.

Bonhoeffer did more than write words about seeing crises as a time for personal growth. His life and death are magnificent tributes to the reality about which he wrote. A world-renowned theologian as a very young man, he was offered many opportunities to sit out the Second World War as an honored lecturer in the United States, but he insisted on returning to his native Germany to be with his family and fellow citizens. There he organized an underground seminary. Later he was arrested for conspiring to assassinate Adolph Hitler—an involvement that was contrary to his own theological convictions but which he chose to make under the circumstances. Confined for two years in a Nazi concentration camp, he was executed at the special order of Himmler just a few days before Allied forces liberated that camp.

All during his captivity, Bonhoeffer served as a source of strength and hope to his fellow prisoners.

> In prison and concentration camps, Bonhoeffer greatly inspired by his indomitable courage, his unselfishness and his goodness, all those who came into contact with him. He even inspired his guards with respect, some of whom became so attached to him that they smuggled out of prison his papers and poems written there, and apologized to him for having to lock his doors after the round in the courtyard.[8]

Those writings have been published and are among the most treasured writings in theology today. One of those poems he called "Who Am I?" It speaks of the struggles going on in his soul—struggles with himself, with his self-image, his sense of self-worth. Notice how he listened to and dealt with what other people were saying about him. Notice how his own inner

[8] Reprinted with the permission of Macmillan Publishing Company from *The Cost of Discipleship* by Deitrich Bonhoeffer, translated from the German by R. H. Fuller. Copyright © 1959 by SCM Press. Page 14.

feelings and fears mocked him, belittled him, made him wonder about himself. Surely if this brilliant, brave, and deeply committed human being could face up to and admit to such struggles within himself, there is hope for all of us in our struggles with these same forces, from without and from within.

Who am I? They often tell me
I stepped from my cell's confinement
calmly, cheerfully, firmly,
like a Squire from his country house.

Who Am I? They often tell me
I used to speak to my warders
freely and friendly and clearly,
as though it were mine to command.

Who Am I? They also tell me
I bore the days of misfortune
equably, smilingly, proudly,
like one accustomed to win.

Am I then really that which other men tell of?
Or am I only what I myself know of myself?
Restless and longing and sick, like a bird in a cage,
struggling for breath, as though hands were
      compressing my throat,
yearning for colors, for flowers, for the voices of
      birds,
thirsting for words of kindness, for neighborliness,
tossing in expectation of great events,
powerlessly trembling for friends at an infinite
      distance,
weary and empty at praying, at thinking, at making,
faint and ready to say farewell to it all.

Who am I? This or the Other?
Am I one person today and tomorrow another?
Am I both at once? A hypocrite before others,
and before myself a contemptible woebegone weakling?
Or is something within me still like a beaten army
fleeing in disorder from victory already achieved?

Who Am I? They mock me, these lonely questions of
  mine.
Whoever I am, Thou knowest, O God, I am thine![9]

Bonhoeffer listened to and was obviously pleased by the
positive comments made about him by fellow prisoners. He
valued the community of support around him. He took these
affirmations into himself and allowed them to add to his sense
of personal richness. He didn't reject this part of his being as
false pride, nor did he use it as a defense against hearing the
pain and fear that lived inside of him. He accepted himself as
being a strong and hopeful and helpful source of strength to
others.

His inner sense of his own worth gave him the courage to
endure the pain of being in touch also with his feelings of
despair and hopelessness. He was explicit in writing down the
fine things others said about him. Then he was even more
explicit in describing his longings, pains, exhaustion, and
feelings of powerlessness. He did not hide or deny or make
excuses for the psychological anguish that contradicted his
preferred self-image.

With remarkable fortitude, he looked at both sides of his
human condition. He recognized and accepted the paradoxical reality of both sides of himself: the "little lower than the
angels" self and the self that was as weak and powerless as a
grasshopper. He courageously confronted and examined
these apparent contradictions and the painful struggles they
set off within him.

Finally, Bonhoeffer revealed the source of the courage
that allowed him to face those mocking and lonely questions.
He said to his God, "I am Thine!" *He chose to believe that he
was loved.* He believed he was loved with a love from which
nothing, not even the depravities of a concentration camp nor
the looming possibility of a violent death, could separate him.

---

[9] Ibid, p. 15ff.

Who was he in the midst of all the pains of the world and his own internal contradictions? He was a worthwhile human being. He believed he was loved!

Bonhoeffer's confidence was grounded in his faith (and faith is the only way that anyone ever receives love) in the God he believed to be revealed in Jesus Christ. In the poem he presents this faith as the end result of his struggles, and I'm sure that it was. On the other hand, I'm equally certain Bonhoeffer would not have been able to undertake the struggle, to face all that inner turmoil and to write it down, if that faith decision had not been made many times in the past. His faith supported his painful self-examination.

The courage to be oneself, which is a prime characteristic of healthy self-esteem, is also the quality that makes it possible. As May highlighted, that courage arises from "one's sense of dignity and self-esteem." And where do that dignity and self-esteem come from? I am convinced that they come from faith—from the decision to believe, and to act on the belief, that we are loved.

If Bonhoeffer had allowed his self-esteem, his sense of personal richness, to depend on the people or circumstances around him, he would have been devastated by being captured and imprisoned by the Nazis. If he had chosen to build his sense of himself on the fine things others said about him, it would have been impossible for him to face the totally contradictory experiences of fear, pain, longing, and powerlessness going on inside of him.

He did not allow his self-esteem to become other-esteem. He took personal responsibility for his sense of worth. He chose to believe that he was loved. Faith is never a habit. It is a decision that must be made again and again. Even when the circumstances around him day after day after day seemed to scream that it was not true, Bonhoeffer continued clinging to that sense of himself. Even though he was a prisoner, with his physical freedom denied almost totally, he continued to reach into himself and to find there the sense of personal richness that allowed him to cope with his torment. He did more than cope. He found the incredible freedom to make his life a source of hope and inspiration to others.

This remarkable courage is by no means the exclusive domain of Christians. The great Jewish psychologist Viktor Frankl, also a World War II concentration camp prisoner, reported similar experiences in his classic book, *Man's Search for Meaning.* This is a man who speaks from three years in concentrations camps, nearly all spent in slave labor and in conditions of near starvation.

> We who lived in concentration camps can remember the men who walked through the huts comforting others, giving away their last piece of bread. They may have been few in number, but they offer sufficient proof that everything can be taken from a man but one thing: the last of the human freedoms— to choose one's attitude in any given set of circumstances, to choose one's own way.[10]

Choosing one's own way occupies a central place in the dignity and worth of being human. As parents, we must hold this as our dearest hope for our children: to love them so consistently and unconditionally that they learn to trust in their inherent capability, lovability, and worth. As responsible persons on our own, this must be our goal for ourselves: to take responsibility for our lives, to create and pursue our own expectations, to nurture our deepest selves.

When we truly value ourselves, we are able to forgive ourselves and to see possibilities for growth in every experience, no matter how painful it may be. We now turn our attention to how this change happens.

---

[10] Viktor Frankl, *Man's Search for Meaning* (Boston: Beacon Press, 1959), p. 65.

CHAPTER FIVE

Change Follows Acceptance

New lives for old! New lives for old! That's been the cry of the church for twenty centuries—and for good reason. The church claims to be the living body of one who made the extraordinary promise, "I have come that you might have life and have it more abundantly." The promises of change and growth are central to the Christian faith. Paul Scherer, one of the most famous Lutheran preachers of this century, once said something to the effect that if the church can't make good on the promise of a new life, it probably can't make good on any of its claims.

For many of us who grew up in the church and cut our theological teeth on those words of hope, that promised new life now seems to have about as much substance as the luminous castles on the distant horizon at the beginning of the Disney TV shows. The distance between us and that appealing but elusive new life seems to keep increasing and turning into a veritable no-man's-land strewn with the scars of years of repeated defeats, disappointments, and disillusionments.

It's not just religious people who want a new beginning, a new opportunity, a new life that is fuller and richer and finer: with more love, more joy, more vitality, more freedom, more self-confidence and self-respect, more satisfaction and meaning. We all want a new chance at that more abundant life. Our repeated failures to attain it have left many of us so despairing and cynical that we laugh about the nonsense of making new year's resolutions, as if sharing a joke with the rest of humanity about the illusion of really changing. Many still talk a good game about change and growth, but few people live in the confidence that this longed-for new life will ever really happen.

Most of us were taught that change and growth are achieved by discipline and determination. I got this message from my family, my teachers in various schools, people at church, my athletic coaches, and my employers. This ethic pervades the country in which I was born and in whose military I served, and the society whose truths and traditions I absorbed. Everyone seemed absolutely certain that people change for the better by dint of effort—and usually by being compelled by some outside force.

What makes this teaching so deceptive is that it *is* half true, and it *does* produce some results. Some causal connection does exist between how much one studies and the grades one receives, between exercise and good health, between hard work and tasks accomplished. The longer we stay in the field, the more land we can plow, usually—unless the equipment breaks down or we drive into a ditch in the dark.

But that half truth, without the other half, becomes not true at all. Though endorsed and taught by most churches, that approach to change contradicts any notion that faith might be involved. Instead, the message usually is that successful change depends not on what we believe about the love of God or our own lovability/capability, but on our determination to quit doing "bad" things and begin doing "good" ones. As those of us who have tried to be less selfish or more conscientious can tell you, this approach is not only unsuccessful in producing the desired change, it sublimates so much of who we are that we can no longer make many necessary and important decisions about our behavior.

The one who first opened my eyes to how constructive and positive growth occurs was Carl Rogers, one of the most influential psychologists of the past fifty years. His writings pointed me in the direction in which positive change is to be found.

> I shall assume a constant and optimal set of conditions for facilitating this change. . . . For our present purpose I believe I can state this assumed condition in one word. . . . the client experiences himself as being fully *received*. By this I mean that whatever his feelings—fear, despair, insecurity, anger, whatever his mode of expression—silence, gestures, tears, or words; whatever he finds himself being in this moment, he senses that he is psychologically *received*, just as he is, by the therapist.[1]

Rogers' phrase, "being fully received," opened a door through which I gained access to the heart and soul of my own heritage. Bit by bit, certain Bible verses I'd memorized as a child and carried in some cold storage vault within me came alive with personal meaning and hope.

> "Let the children come to me, and do not hinder them; for to such belongs the kingdom of heaven." [Matthew 19:14]

> "Come to me, all who labor and are heavy laden, and I will give you rest." [Matthew 11:28]

> But while he was yet at a distance, his father saw him and had compassion, and ran and embraced him and kissed him. [Luke 15:20b]

Rogers realized that people in therapy make positive changes in their lives when they experience themselves being accepted just as they are by the therapist. They grow not when they are bribed or hounded or shamed or silenced or shown to be mistaken or wrong or lazy but when they are accepted.

Acceptance is not the same as approval, nor does it imply any lack of desire to change. Being accepted means being acknowledged for who I am and what I am at this moment. The accepting person or therapist may not agree with what I think or how I behave, but he or she does not shame or reject me. My right and responsibility to make the choices that affect my life are respected. I feel myself welcomed, respected, valued, taken seriously. Within the warmth of that acceptance, I do not feel pressured to defend or explain. This leaves me free to take an honest look at myself and examine the truth of who and what I am and how I came to be that way.

Alcoholics, to use a well-known and obvious example, are prisoners of their addiction so long as they deny their condition. Indeed, denial becomes the consuming endeavor of their lives: They refuse to acknowledge any serious need to change. So the choice of changing doesn't even exist for them. Only as they accept their condition can they put themselves in a position to make constructive changes.

This is not dissimilar to the situation of a good friend of mine who died two months after he was diagnosed with cancer. His wife said he'd had various physical ailments for a couple of years but refused to go to the doctor. She thought he probably feared he might have cancer and didn't want to deal with that frightening possibility. If he had gone to the doctor and faced up to his condition, chances are that treatment

---

[1] Carl Rogers, *On Becoming A Person,* © 1961 by Houghton Mifflin Company. Reprinted by permission of the publisher.

would have been successful. His lack of acceptance sent him off to an early death. The point is that we cannot deal with a problem until we acknowledge its existence. Acceptance is an absolutely essential condition for change.

Shortly after the wonder and excitement and good sense of this important truth began to stir within me, I realized something almost as astounding as the first discovery. It was this: *Rogers' magnificent insight, that change follows acceptance, has always been a core element of the Christian gospel.* This understanding is the very foundation for the biblical story of God's action in Jesus Christ. "While we were yet sinners"—that is, having done nothing to earn or deserve God's favor—"Christ died for us" (Romans 5:8)—that is, made the ultimate sacrifice of his life as an expression of the unlimited and unconditional nature of God's love for us. God does not require people to change to some predetermined level of goodness to receive him, his love, his mercy, or his blessings. On the contrary, God takes the initiative to come to us, gently and vulnerably and lovingly, just where we are and just as we are. Receiving us fully as we are, he pours out the fullness of his acceptance and forgiveness and love.

Nowhere have I found this understanding expressed more profoundly or precisely than in a remarkable little book, *A Life to Live, A Way to Pray,* by Father John Coburn. Formerly the Dean of the Episcopal Seminary in Cambridge, Massachusetts, he was the rector of St. James' Church in New York City when he wrote this book. It has the beautiful simplicity that reflects a deep and personal understanding of a monumental truth.

> . . . the key is acceptance of ourselves, our circumstances, our relationships just as they are. It does not mean they will not change. *It does mean that change follows acceptance.* I can change for the better only after I have accepted myself at my worst. . . . If we are to work things through in our lives, we can do so only as we accept those things as

> the raw material of life which God has "placed in
> our hands" for the purpose of living [emphasis
> added].[2]

The New Testament message is that God gives us total
and unconditional acceptance. We no longer need to justify
ourselves or make ourselves look good, which we could do
only by comparison. Comparison creates alienation and strife.
Instead, we may accept God's acceptance and believe that we
are loved. We then have the freedom to look at and acknowledge what we need to change in our lives and to make those
changes. We can move toward becoming those persons we
were created to be and which, within ourselves, we long to be.
A new life is possible. An effort on our part is required. But
the beginning of this new life is faith: the risky willingness to
believe we are loved.

Some religious people object that this makes it sound
too easy; but, in many ways, accepting acceptance is the most
difficult challenge of all. Years ago I saw a TV drama in which
the female protagonist recounted how, as a young woman in
Germany during the Second World War, she was consistently
used and abused by soldiers. For many years thereafter she
had a recurring dream in which she had given birth to an idiot
child who then pursued her throughout the dream. The woman
spent all of her time running away, trying to escape. Finally,
she said, the day came when she stopped running. She turned
around, took the child into her arms, and kissed him. In
recounting this experience to a friend, she explained, "That
child was my life."

Though I remember nothing else about the story, that
small segment has lived on in memory. It fits so well. We
spend tremendous effort and energy trying to run away from
those parts of ourselves that shame and embarrass us, deny-

---

[2] John Coburn, *A Life to Live, A Way to Pray* (New York: Seabury
Press, 1973), pp. 26–27.

ing any thoughts and behaviors that contradict our self-image. Our personalities become significantly shaped by what we deny. We construct a personality and a lifestyle to hide whatever it is we cannot accept. People who long for the closeness they needed but never received as children, who yearn for the warmth of a human touch, frequently show themselves to the world as rigid and cold, sometimes as vigorous critics of anything sexual.

Denied parts of us do not go away. They continue pursuing us, exhausting us, and distorting our way of living and working and relating to others. This continues until we quit running, turn around, and accept those parts of ourselves. Then, like the woman in the drama, we find our lives. Change follows acceptance.

But is the change real? Or is this just another spiritual smoke screen, a religious illusion? The Apollo High School in Simi Valley, California provides us with an assuringly real example that acceptance is, indeed, the essential condition for human change. For openers, Apollo has the most unusual mission statement I've ever seen attached to a public school:

> The mission of Apollo High School is for students, staff, parents, and community to form a partnership in education dedicated to fostering self-esteem in students.

This school does not exist to get its students into college or even graduated. Nor is its faculty committed to teach certain social values or keep kids off the street. The school's whole focus is to foster self-esteem.

Apollo is a continuation school, which means its students haven't been able to make it in the regular high schools, for a variety of reasons They have fallen through the cracks of the educational structure and are not, ostensibly, prime candidates for high self-esteem. Of the students entering Apollo over a period of more than fifteen years:

80% had missed over 70% of their classes the previous semester.

60% had failed two or more classes the previous semester.

50% were working two or more grade levels below their ability.

80% used drugs on a weekly basis.

30% were on probation.

30% came from alcoholic family backgrounds.

20% had attempted suicide.

Here's what happens to them at Apollo, the school whose mission it is to foster self-esteem in its students:

86% graduate (in a state where just under 70% graduate from all high schools).

78% improve in attendance.

5% are on probation, after one year.

20% use drugs on a weekly basis, after one year. (This figure continues to decrease if the students stay on at Apollo for more than a year.)

When asked how he accounts for the dramatic changes that take place in the lives of these kids who couldn't make it elsewhere, principal Brad Greene said Apollo's program is based on the conviction that it should be fun to come to school. In his words, the key to success at Apollo is "committed, caring teachers who communicate effectively with students in an environment of cooperation."

Greene uses another alliterative motto to explain what he feels all students need to experience: Attention, Acceptance, Appreciation, and Affection.

Students get attention in either negative or positive ways. Students need to be accepted, forget

> their past, start fresh. Students need to be ap-
> preciated through their learning styles, and love is
> the most powerful force in helping others.

What happens at Apollo sounds very much like a spiritual experience. In its deepest sense, I believe it is—even though it takes place in a thoroughly secular structure without the assistance of any ordained clergy. The truth of the gospel continues to be true whether it is experienced in a religious setting or out in the world. Apollo's record shows that we too can forget the past by letting go of failures and mistakes, the memories of which continue to haunt us. We can forget about them once we have accepted, examined, dealt with, and forgiven ourselves for making them. When we deal with our past in this responsible way, we no longer have to defend it, hide from it, or make up for it. Those memories no longer plague us. We are thus able to start fresh. Acceptance gives us the freedom to make a new beginning, to grow into a new life.

The Apostle Paul speaks of forgetting the past in a similar way in his letter to the Philippians (Philippians 3:12–14). After describing the new life to which he aspires, he says:

> Not that I have already obtained this or am already
> perfect; but I press on to make it my own because
> Christ Jesus has made me his own. . . . One thing I
> do, forgetting what lies behind and straining for-
> ward to what lies ahead, I press on toward the goal
> for the prize of the upward call of God in Christ
> Jesus.

Because of his conviction that "Christ Jesus has made me his own"—that is, has accepted and loved him just as he is—Paul is able to acknowledge his position. He has not yet attained to his goal, but he is able to let go of the failures and disappointments that lie behind him and to press on to an ever fuller realization of that loving purpose for which he was given life.

Students at Apollo experience positive and hopeful changes as they are released from the failures of their past and encouraged to take responsibility for their present and future lives. The program at Apollo has shown that fostering self-esteem by giving students attention, acceptance, appreciation, and affection accomplishes the academic goals to which all schools aspire but which fewer and fewer are achieving. Surely now, when education is one of our most critical national problems, it is time for us to incorporate these findings into the whole educational enterprise, as well as into our individual lives.

So far as the words go, the church and Christian people have always known the promise and power of acceptance as a condition of change. Though we keep losing sight of them, the first recorded words out of Jesus' mouth in the earliest of the gospels were: "The time is fulfilled, and the kingdom of God is at hand; repent, and believe in the gospel."

Repent means to turn about and go in an opposite direction. For instance, quit looking for a new life through honors and achievements. Let go of any negative images of yourself and your sense of failure. "Believe in the gospel" means to believe the good news: that you are accepted and forgiven and loved.

Change follows acceptance. The simplicity of that truth is deceptive, for two reasons. First, it means accepting that we are accepted. No one has ever expressed that more beautifully or more accurately than did Paul Tillich in his famous sermon, "You Are Accepted."

> You are accepted. *You are accepted,* accepted by that which is greater than you, and the name of which you do not know. Do not ask for the name now; perhaps you will find it later. Do not try to do

> anything now; perhaps later you will do much. Do
> not seek for anything; do not perform anything; do
> not intend anything. *Simply accept the fact that you
> are accepted!* ... And nothing is demanded of this
> experience, no religious or moral or intellectual
> presupposition, nothing but *acceptance*.[3]

Acceptance is what Rogers understood as the first and most important function of the therapist: providing clients with a warm, welcome, caring, nonjudgmental, safe environment within which to take an honest look at themselves. This makes it possible for clients to gain new and more accurate understandings of themselves and their behavior. It also allows them to make new and more realistic decisions about how to think and act.

Giving acceptance is all the therapist can do. It's all the faculty at Apollo High School can do. In fact, it is all God can do. If we are to change, then we must be willing to accept acceptance.

The second difficulty is that we must then accept ourselves. It takes a great deal of discipline and determination—and hard work, conscientious commitment, and vigorous perseverance—to accept ourselves. How can we accept actions and qualities that we have learned to abhor? How can we accept what we have spent our lives believing to be obviously and utterly unacceptable? How can we accept in ourselves what our parents and our society have labeled "selfish" and "evil"?

It cannot be done easily—not by anyone. And it cannot be done at all, I believe, *unless we have first experienced the miracle of acceptance from some other human being.* We may

---

[3] Reprinted with permission of Charles Scribner's Sons, an imprint of Macmillan, Inc. from *The Shaking of the Foundations* by Paul Tillich. Copyright © 1948 Charles Scribner's Sons; copyright renewed © 1976 Hannah Tillich.

feel it from a counselor or a pastor or a special friend or people in a nurturing community. Once we have experienced it, the door opens to a new and fuller life. And once that door has opened, the responsibility is ours to step through it: to accept acceptance and to accept ourselves.

At one of the hundreds of conferences I attented as a pastor, I met a remarkably competent and compassionate clergyman, "Dave," from the Midwest, the part of the country where I grew up. I was impressed by his personal warmth, the clarity of his insights, and the vitality and sensitivity with which he described his ministry. Years later, I happened to mention Dave in a conversation with another pastor who was a neighbor and friend of mine. As it turns out, my friend had been the pastor in the small Midwestern town where Dave had been born. He had known Dave's family well.

Dave was born in the 1930s to an unwed mother. Being single and pregnant in a small town in the Midwest was not nearly so common or accepted then as it is today. But the church of which Dave's mother was a member accepted her as she was; and, when he was born, they accepted Dave. Those people surrounded that young woman and her son with loving, nurturing support, which allowed the two of them to accept themselves, to grow, and to live worthwhile and fulfilling lives. Their lives had meaning for them and great benefit for others. The acceptance given and accepted by real people resulted in growth and an extension of love far beyond that community.

Change follows acceptance, and self-acceptance follows acceptance by others. The hard work that change first requires of us is to accept acceptance. The word for that hard work is *faith*. And what is it we are to believe? Writing from a medical perspective, Bernie Siegel has provided the same message as the good news of the gospel, in words that go straight to the heart: 'You are not that unloved child anymore."

The critical importance of faith is not restricted to Christians or those who think of themselves as religious. Everyone believes something. Before Columbus, the greatest minds in the world believed the earth was flat. They had no proof, except what they saw with their own eyes: a world that certainly looked flat. So they believed what their eyes seemed to reveal, and their faith controlled and restricted their lives: their thinking, their imaginations, their behavior.

People's beliefs still control their lives. If we believe we are unlovable and incapable of productive living, we will avoid or ignore evidence to the contrary. If we believe we are stuck with being the way we are and cannot change, we won't. If we believe life has no meaning—and we can recite all kinds of evidence to support our beliefs that it does not, including events we have seen with our own eyes—then those beliefs will define and control our lives. Carl Jung put it like this: "It all depends on how we look at things, and not on how they are in themselves."[4]

How we choose to look at things is determined by what we believe; what we believe determines what we see. What we believe is our choice. It's that portion of what's happening that is under our control, and for which we must be willing to take full responsibility.

It was the faith of the biblical writers, for example, that gave them a distinctive way of looking at things. Look, for instance, at the exodus out of Egypt, which was the pivotal event in the entire Old Testament. Everything else in the Old Testament was written later and looks back on that event as the basis for its perspective. The people of Israel had been slaves of the Egyptians for 430 years. Their captivity is

---

[4] Quoted by Bernie Siegel in *Peace, Love and Healing* (New York: Harper & Row, 1989), p. 153.

historical reality, which does not change. The fact that they got out and eventually made it to another land, a "promised land" in which they established their home, is another unchanging historical event. But how did it happen? How did they get out? How you answer depends on how you choose to look at it.

The biblical writers chose to believe that God acted within history to set his people free. They wrote of a captive, helpless people who were delivered from the might and power of the Egyptian pharaoh by the direct intervention of God himself. They saw God's action symbolized in plagues and in the people's crossing of the Red Sea. That way of looking makes all the difference in how the story is told.

It has made all the difference to millions of people for thousands of years. People live in a particular way when they believe that a loving, caring God acts to set people free. They live in a different way when they believe it's all up to them, that the only help they're ever going to get is what they can do for themselves. People who view the world from the faith perspective of a loving, acting-in-the-world God find the courage to hang in there when everything around them seems to offer no hope at all. Like Bonhoeffer, they believe they are loved, which gives them a different view of themselves and allows a different response to life.

Everything in the New Testament was written after the crucifixion and ressurection of Jesus. Those pivotal events give foundation and meaning to everything else in the New Testament. That Jesus was killed is an historical reality, but what happened after that is a matter of how you look at it. The New Testament writers believed Jesus was raised from the dead and that he later appeared to many of his followers. Because of the faith aroused in them by their experience of the resurrected, living Jesus, these beaten, defeated followers became such a fearless, dynamic force that they created a new fellowship called the *church*. The community generated by faith in the resurrection has outlived the Roman Empire and has continued spreading throughout the world for two thousand years.

In the midst of the many failures and deaths we all experience in the course of our living, people who believe in a God of resurrections live with a remarkable confidence and hope. They're not stuck with being dead or finished. There is always hope for new life.

According to the Bible, the resurrected Jesus never appeared to any nonbeliever. Some may choose to see that as evidence that the story of the ressurrection was simply a conspiracy by his followers. Perhaps it was. It is also possible, however, to interpret this fact in another way: as another indication that our response determines our reality. Perhaps only those who believed in his love were able to experience his living reality.

In his second book, Bernie Siegel writes:

> While pessimists have a more accurate view of the world, optimists live a lot longer and have a better time. So, in the end, both can be said to have seen the truth about their own lives—in fact, to have created that truth.[5]

Those who believe God raised Jesus from the dead can live with the confidence that the love of God is active within the world, even in such harsh and seemingly final realities as death. A classic expression of this faith was written by the apostle Paul in his letter to the Romans (Romans 8:38, 39):

> For I am sure that neither death, nor life, nor angels, nor principalities, nor things present, nor

---

[5] Bernie Siegel, *Peace, Love and Healing* (New York: Harper & Row 1989), p. 169.

> things to come, nor powers, nor height, nor depth,
> nor anything else in all creation, will be able to
> separate us from the love of God in Christ Jesus
> our Lord.

When someone who knows us and all about us and everything we have done and said and thought accepts us, then the
possibility exists for us to accept ourselves. The Christian
faith says this has happened, for all of us: that the God of all
creation, who knows us inside and out, accepts and forgives
and loves us. His is a love from which nothing can ever separate us. Having faith in this acceptance allows us to change
and grow.

The gospel story is that God communicated that love to
the world through the human life of Jesus of Nazareth. Jesus
instructed his followers to be the human beings through
whom that love will continue to be communicated into the
world. The story continues as the human beings who now
compose Christ's body—the church—allow God's unconditional love to be made known through them to the people and
the structures of the world today. Those of us who read and
accept the scriptural story have reason to expect that this will
happen, and all of us have a desperate need for it to happen.
So we become massively disappointed, hurt, angry, even
despairing when it does not. But we are also responsible if it
does not. Only those who accept acceptance are able to extend
that life-giving acceptance to others.

Ernest Becker, a consummate scholar from a Jewish
background, has read deeply and with understanding from
most all the great thinkers in psychology and philosophy. He
develops convincing evidence that life is so mysterious, so
unpredictable, so terrifying that no one can face it and be a
part of it without some sort of "illusion":

> What is the ideal for mental health, then? A lived,
> compelling illusion that does not lie about life,
> death and reality; one honest enough to follow its

own commandments: I mean, not to kill, not to take the lives of others to jusfity itself. [The psychologist Otto] Rank saw Christianity as a truly great ideal foolishness in the sense that we have been discussing it: a childlike trust and hope for the human condition that left open the realm of mystery.[6]

Viewing Christianity from the outside, Becker recognized its potential as a superb avenue for creating the highest possible expression of a truly human life. Then, sad to say, Becker felt compelled to write this next sentence:

Obviously, all religions fall far short of their own ideals, and Rank was talking abut Christianity not as practiced but as an ideal.

Having experienced the pain and disappointment of Christianity as it is often practiced, many people in cynical despair abandon the whole notion of a spiritual faith. That position proves to be highly unworkable and unsatisfying also. Fortunately, the truth of the Christian ideal is not totally enclosed within dusty tombs and distant cathedrals. Occasionally along the way our lives are touched by people who, though they may not have understood or cared about any of the words of the scriptures or spiritual writers, spent their lives "living and doing in a partly self-forgetful way." Those people make all the difference. The gospel that came into the world with a human face and hands and heart at Bethlehem comes alive through the personal presence and touch of loving human beings today.

From those who have known us and accepted us, we have received a gift. They have given us the chance to have a life with some meaning, some hope, some joy, some fleeting ex-

---

[6] From *The Denial of Death* by Ernest Becker. Copywright © 1973 by The Free Press, a Division of Macmillan, Inc. Reprinted by permission of the publisher.

periences of love. These are not the people who lie to create an illusory world of their own choosing. They are people who have chosen to believe that, in spite of all the evidence to the contrary, there's a caring, loving heart at the center of all existence. In this faith they have chosen to live, to accept the gift of life, and to accept us as a part of that gift. Accepting themselves allows them to accept us. Accepting their acceptance allows us to accept ourselves.

Acceptance can give us a whole new perspective on ourselves, on life, and on the people around us. Within that new way of looking, we are able to respond differently to the events that make up our worlds. That different response can be to grow. Faith is what allows us to change—faith to believe that we are not unloved children and faith enough to act in ways that are appropriate to that new understanding. And the result of our different responses is a new life—our growth can be a new life.

Once I heard the well-known author Frederick Buechner speak of his conviction that a saint may be a criminally or morally reprehensible person; but above all else, that person is a life-giver. "If a saint touches your life," Buechner said, "you come alive in a new way."

Change follows acceptance, not the other way around. Change follows our acknowledgment that we are accepted, that we are persons of worth, that we have an important contribution to make to the lives of others. When we accept ourselves, we can let go of guilt and shame. We can find hope and meaning.

"You are not that unloved child any more." Do you believe it?

CHAPTER SIX

Responsibility

In discussions concerning self-esteem, nothing has proven more surprising to most people than this: taking responsibility for ones's own feelings, decisions, and behavior is an essential condition for developing healthy self-esteem. People who are not willing or able to take responsibility for their own actions and behavior simply cannot have a healthy sense of themselves as significant, capable, self-actualizing human beings. Men and women who enjoy healthy self-esteem do not wait for others to make them happy. They take responsibility for their own lives.

In his work with cancer patients, for example, Bernie Siegel found that people who stand up for themselves are better able to fight their disease. They are also more resistant to disease in the first place. Choosing to affirm ourselves as worthwhile human beings is necessarily a choice to take responsibility for our own existence. Choosing between low self-esteem and high self-esteem means choosing between helplessness and responsibility. As Siegel says:

> We can teach people not to be helpless, we can teach them to be fighters, and in even the most

> desperate of circumstances we can still help them
> find the will to live.[1]

Many of us have difficulty coping with life and relationships and ourselves as adults. Most of us actually learned to
be helpless in the environments in which we grew up as
children. Parents who feel overwhelmed by life provide a
model of helplessness for their children. Sometimes this
sense of being overwhelmed shows up in obvious dependency
and "poor little me" behaviors. In other situations, the fear of
life may be equally profound but the expression may be very
subtle, showing itself in less blatant attitudes and veiled
insinuations.

This understanding first came to my attention almost
twenty years ago through Wayne Dyer's book, *Your Erroneous
Zones*. Up to that time in my life it was second nature for me to
say things such as "We'd have a happy home and a pleasant
time around here if you kids would just shape up!" In reflection, I realized that the environment in which I had been
reared was full of such phrases—and the attitude they reflect.
Through those experiences I had learned to blame other
people when things aren't going the way I wanted them to go.
That became my perception of reality. It seemed clear to me
that life would be wonderful if those other people would just
think and behave in the way they should.

Dyer changed all that for me. His point was that we are
the ones who choose how we will feel and respond in any given
situation. If we say, "You make me so angry" or "You make
me so happy," we deny our choices. No one else makes us
happy or sad or anything else. We must take responsibility for
our own feelings. If I am angry, it is because I have chosen to
be angry. I could have chosen to be sad or amused or frightened

---

[1] Bernie Siegel, *Peace, Love and Healing* (New York: Harper & Row,
1989), p. 27.

or shocked or something else. Even to say, "You make me so happy" is to give someone else the power to determine who and what I am going to be. It is different to say, "I feel delighted, so glad to be alive, when I am with you."

As long as we go around blaming other people or events for our unhappiness, we adopt a position of helplessness. We think of our happiness or unhappiness as something beyond our control, something that only someone else can affect. We become helpless victims.

As obvious as all this may seem when it is written out, it is one of the most difficult attitude adjustments I have ever undertaken. Up to that point, it had never occurred to me that I possessed a victim mentality. Acknowledging that perspective within me was an especially painful process. It was not how I wanted to picture myself at all; yet, examining my life as an adult, it was true. I'd learned that way of thinking through words and concepts and experiences in my environment. It seemed perfectly normal. My beliefs and expectations had hardened into conviction. It became my normal way of looking at life and at myself. Undetected and resolved, my victim mentality sabotaged my efforts to grow and become a responsible adult.

The "victim" way of looking at life blinds us to our options. Sometimes we even hear ourselves using the words "I had no choice," or "He left me no alternative," or "Anyone in my position would have done exactly the same." These words portray an attitude towards ourselves: that we are without power or the opportunity to make decisions about what affects our lives and behavior. Living from that perspective, our lives become both hopeless and boring. We just go through life mechanically, doing what we must without recognizing the freedom or opportunity for it to be otherwise.

By the time I finished reading and reflecting on Dyer's ideas, I started to see and understand and believe that I could take responsibility for my own happiness or unhappiness. I wanted to. Slowly and painfully, I'm managing to transform my thought process. As my beliefs about myself change, so does my behavior. As frightening and difficult as it is, taking responsibility for myself and learning a new way of thinking and believing have been exhilarating. Taking responsibility for my own life allows me to feel some of the power of being alive as an adult, choice-making human being.

Parents with grown up children sometimes feel sorry for themselves when they don't see or hear from their offspring as much as they would like. After all the time and attention they poured out while those youngsters were growing up, parents can easily work up a case for feeling like victims of their children's neglect. For me, moving out of the victim role means accepting full responsibility for my own happiness in the present, understanding that sharing in the adventures of my children's growing was its own reward, and finding satisfaction in knowing that my children are now able to live their own lives and share their love with their own families. What I have is enough. When I get calls and visits from my kids, that's simply frosting on the cake.

The way we're reared gives us a start in one direction or the other: more toward responsibility or more toward helplessness. Whichever way we were pointed as children, as adults we choose our own direction. We choose an identity, a sense of ourselves—either valued or not enough, either responsible or helpless—and that choice determines the health and productivity and satisfaction of our experience of being alive. Even in so severe a situation as a serious illness, the attitude of helplessness or responsibility taken by the person with the disease is of major significance. Siegel reports, "One's attitude toward oneself is the single most important factor in healing and staying well."[2]

---

[2] Bernie Siegel, *Love, Medicine and Miracles* (New York: Harper & Row, 1986), p. 76.

Self-esteem is a choice that all human beings make. To refuse to accept the responsibility of making it as an adult is to choose helplessness by default.

This necessity to choose was portrayed dramatically in the life of Jesus. Each of the first three Gospels (Matthew, Mark, and Luke) reports a major choice-making experience called "The Three Temptations." The story dramatizes the choices Jesus was forced to make at the very beginning of his ministry. Even he could not become a functioning adult without going through the painful ordeal of taking responsibility for his own life, choosing for himself what his self-image and the source of his security, worth, and power would be.

As recorded in the fourth chapter of the Gospel according to Matthew, this story is one of the most significant and insightful descriptions of taking personal responsiblity I've ever read. It is filled with some incredibly astute and thoroughly contemporary insights into the process through which we become authentic and capable human beings, able to take responsibility for ourselves. In the first place, the timing of these temptations is profoundly significant. Jesus is tempted immediately after his baptism, and the baptism narrative focuses on Jesus' identification with the people. Matthew emphasizes that *all* the people from the entire region had gone to John to be baptized, and Jesus took his place in line as one of them. He did not place himself above the others, not in his mind and not in his actions. He took his place as a member of the human race. All human beings are together in our responsiblity to choose who we are, or whose we are.

At the moment of Jesus' baptism, "the heavens were opened" and a voice from heaven said, "This is my beloved Son, with whom I am well pleased." This shows that Jesus' identity was given to him from outside himself. So it is with all of us, as discussed in earlier chapters. The people who surround us during our growing up give us many (though often contradictory) messages about who we are. Our images of ourselves are not invented out of our imaginations. They are given. From these we choose which ones to adopt as our own self-images.

Up to this point in the story as told by Matthew, Jesus had done absolutely nothing to make himself worthy or deserving of God's favor. Through the first three chapters of Matthew's Gospel, Jesus had done no teaching, no healing, no miracles, no good works of any kind. Matthew thus emphasizes that the identity of sonship to God was given totally from God's initiative and choice. The affirmation of our worth to God is *given,* not earned. I emphasize this consistent New Testament teaching because it is radically different from the assumptions of many religious people today.

It is at this moment, immediately following the baptism and the words from heaven announcing Jesus as the Son of God, that the story tells us: "Then Jesus was led up by the Spirit into the wilderness to be tempted by the devil" (Matthew 4:1). Saying he was led by the Spirit makes it clear that it was helpful and necessary, God's idea, for Jesus to go through the experience of being tempted by the devil. God had given him his positive identity, the assurance that he was a loved person of worth. To make that identity his own, however, Jesus needed to go into the wilderness, a place of loneliness and reflection and suffering. There he would fast for forty days and nights and then be confronted with the necessity to choose for himself what his identity, his source of worth and power, would be. The story is clear that it was God, not the devil, who put Jesus in the position to make those painful, difficult, and necessary choices. Choosing is an essential part of being human. People who never choose their own lives, the identity on which they will depend for their sense of worth and power, spend their lives in a futile attempt to live out someone else's expectations.

The three temptations symbolize classic but misguided sources of "identity." All three profess to be sources of worth and power, and all are recognizable choices even today.

Buried within each of these temptations is the choice between helplessness and responsibility. Underscoring the importance of a person's sense of identity, the devil begins each of the first two temptations with "*If* you are the Son of God . . .." In other words, he asks Jesus to question the positive identity just given to him. Can he believe he is loved? In times of stress, it's common for people to hear "voices" within them or at least deep-seated feelings that question their sense of personal worth. We find ourselves wondering, "Did my parents really love me? Did they love my sister or brother more? Maybe they just said they loved me, but down deep inside they never really did." In fact, we sometimes call these *bedeviling* questions. When the crunch comes, some of the first questions that arise within us are, "Am I really loved and wanted? Am I really a valued person of worth?"

For the first temptation, Satan urges Jesus to turn the stones into bread; this is sometimes referred to as the "temptation to be relevant." As it is today, the world then was full of starving people. Jesus could have proved himself indispensable and gained a great following if he had used his power to give people bread. The devil was saying, "If you think you're so good, so useful, so right, prove it. Be relevant."

People today may say, "Don't give us a lot of fancy words. If you are right and if you are sincere, help us. Feed us. Clothe us." As sensible as these words sound, they conceal deadly traps. First, these are the words of people who are attempting to avoid personal responsibility, wanting someone else to take care of them. Second, basing our own identity and sense of worth on what we produce means treating ourselves like machines rather than humans. If we accept the judgment that we are what we produce, we wear ourselves out in futile, destructive competitions with ourselves and others. We feel driven to continue producing in order to feel worthwhile and accepted. Our fears compel us to cover up any signs of weakness, loss of power, or aging.

Jesus did not deny the importance of bread. Instead he showed that valuing oneself is even more crucial than an obvious life necessity: "One does not live by bread alone, but on every word that proceeds from the mouth of God" (Matthew 4:4). God spoke words of love and Jesus chose to nurture his being on those words, to find his security and worth and power through faith in that love. He chose to believe that he was loved, and this formed the basis for his identity and his sense of worth.

This does not suggest that being relevant or helping others in need is not important. On the contrary, it is precisely those people whose sense of worth is not in what they produce but in themselves who are the most productive and the most sensitive to others. Their energy is not drained away by the need to prove themselves or to win the favor of others. They are free to act in the most productive ways possible precisely because their worth is already secure, which releases them to place their energy and attention on what needs to be done.

After raising the question of doubt the second time ("If you are the Son of God") the devil suggested a religious forum. If Jesus were to throw himself down from the parapet of the temple, God would have to make good on his promise and rescue him in some dramatic fashion. This would, in turn, give Jesus prominence by gaining for him the attention and admiration of the people. This is sometimes called "the temptation to be spectacular."

The allure of being spectacular has hardly lessened in our day. We frequently use statistics and ratings as measures of worth. They are often our measure of truth as well, in churches as much as in the world. When preachers get together, the conversation frequently turns to: Who has the most spectacular church buildings, the biggest budgets and choirs, the largest worshipping congregation and/or television audience, the most services on Sunday morning? How many people have we converted to our way of thinking?

Strange questions from an institution that traces its origins to a man who assembled a handful of the least prestigous remnants of his society to be his companions and fellow workers. In virtually every part of our lives, we have fallen into the mindset of those who use popularity charts to determine the best soap, books, records, movies, cars, speakers, companies, and leaders.

All this reflects a fragile sense of identity that believes, "If I am not spectacular, I am nothing. To be a person of worth, I must be wanted and popular and, I hope, remembered by generations yet unborn." If we use popularity as the measure of our worth, we are driven to do whatever is necessary to be noticed. Otherwise we risk becoming nothing.

Jesus responded to this temptation by saying, "You must not put the Lord your God to the test." Jesus refused to ask God to prove his love. Asking for proof that we are loved follows from having low self-esteem. If we lack faith in ourselves, we live with a sense of powerlessness. To compensate, we put everyone who loves us to the test: "Prove your love for me. Show me that I am the most important person in your life."

To the extent that we lack confidence in ourselves, we have little to contribute to the lives of others. Instead we pour our energies into proving ourselves and demanding affirmation from others. When we are ruled by negative images of ourselves, even our victories do not nourish our sense of self-worth. Our choice of helplessness continues to prevail. Until we decide to take responsibility for our own lives, and commit ourselves to finding and acquiring a more positive and appropriate self-esteem, our negative sense of ourselves remains unchanged.

Truly productive people are those who choose to believe in themselves. This frees them from anxious needs to be praised and admired. They enjoy authentic words and deeds of appreciation, but they do not depend on other-esteem for their sense of identity or worth. They do not allow others to be in charge of how they're going to feel about themselves. They are free to listen to other people, to see what needs to be done, and to respond to what happens in sensible and effective and responsible ways.

As the final temptation, the devil took Jesus to a high mountain, "and showed him all the kingdoms of the world and the glory of them; and he said to him, 'All these I will give you, if you will fall down and worship me' " (Matthew 4:8–9). This is sometimes called "the temptation to acquire power." Surely we can understand this one! As children of our culture and our time, we begin almost at birth seeking power: the power of attention, wealth, popularity, academic and athletic achievements, influence in high places, business success, high levels of personal competence. We seem convinced that if we have enough power we can do anything, control everything, be absolutely secure. We seem certain that to have some external form of power takes away the devastating pains of our helplessness, but in truth the compulsive search for power reveals the conviction/choice that without an external source of power we are nothing. The insatiable yearning for power is but another reflection of how most of us live: with an unrelenting sense of relative weakness or helplessness, which we use as a ready excuse for failures and disappointments.

Yet, exerting control through the use of power proves to be even more disappointing, especially in the most important areas of our lives, such as personal relationships. Instructed by my patriarchal father-image, for instance, I tried to be a father who exercised unquestioned power over my children. What I discovered was that besides creating constant tensions and strife, my power model was not very effective in accomplishing what needed to be done around the house. Far more importantly for me, it did not achieve what I wanted most deeply: a loving, trusting, sharing relationship with those I loved. Loving relationships grow out of mutual vulnerability, respect, and the sharing of feelings, fears, fantasies, and failures—not from the use of authority, fear, or force.

Using external power to remedy our sense of helplessness is so far off target that even the top "bottom-line, cash-flow" business consultants of our day are assailing it. As a strategy for managing the workplace, it does not work well. Such respected experts as Ken Blanchard and Edward Deming, people whose interest is in production and performance, challenge the effectiveness and practicality of the traditional U.S. business pyramid in which those at the top hold power. Studies have shown that the managers who need to demonstrate power over workers sabotage the process of production and the quality of what is produced. Effective managers are those whose sense of their own worth allows them to let go of their need to control. Their healthy self-esteem enables them to encourage and empower others, to allow people to learn to take responsibility for their lives, and, as Blanchard likes to say, to "help them win."

Similarly, effective counselors are not those who have all the answers and tell people what to do. On the contrary, they accept people as they are and empower them to find the answers and power they have within themselves. They encourage people to take responsibility for their own lives. People with real power are able to give it away rather than using it to protect themselves and to control others.

Jesus answered the temptation for power by saying, "You must worship the Lord your God and serve him alone" (Matthew 4:10).

Satan had offered to give Jesus "all the kingdoms of the world," that is, the power to control; but to receive this power, Jesus had to be willing to be controlled, to bow himself down before Satan. It's something like the mafia, or business corporations, where the "boss" at each successive level within the organization bows down to those above him in the chain of authority in exchange for the right to demand absolute compliance from those beneath him. To receive the power that gives us the right to exercise control, we have to surrender our own freedom and integrity.

Jesus' unwillingness to bow down before Satan was, on the one hand, a refusal to surrender his own freedom and integrity to another. On the other hand, it showed that the authority to control the people of the world was not his goal. God's kingdom is a kingdom of love and love is a choice. Unless it is a freely given choice, it is not love. Jesus chose to believe in God's love as the basis for his own dignity and worth, and he chose to walk the path of love as his means of building the kingdom of God, rather than resorting to coercion or intimidation.

Any attachment to a source of power outside ourselves robs us of our freedom and renders us incapable of entering into fully human relationships. For example, even if my source of power is something so admirable as the Bible, I must defend my interpretation of the Bible to maintain my own sense of authority and well-being. Rather than being an instrument of the love of God, which the God whom I meet in the Bible calls me to be, I become a warrior defending the authority of the Bible—even if that means behaving in some very unloving ways toward those who do not share my point of view. In my dependence on the Bible, I become a slave to words and doctrines and arguments and propositions—and I make myself unapproachable to human beings whenever they disagree. Jesus refused to bow down to anything other than God, and he used his beliefs to get closer to all people, not just followers.

If my sense of power and worth depends on maintaining a particular posture toward the Bible, all who disagree with my interpretation become my enemies—not only to my ideas but also to my worth as a person. Too many Christian missionaries and evangelists have found themselves stuck in precisely that stance. They end up as combantants with precisely those people they went out to woo into a loving relationship with God, contradicting with their lives the message of love on their lips.

When Jesus insisted that God alone is to be worshipped and served, he was choosing the only source of power and worth that sets us free. Even so ancient a Christian document as The Apostles Creed does not affirm a faith in the Bible. Christians believe in the God who reveals himself to them through the persons and events of the Bible. To believe in the God made known to us in Jesus Christ is to believe ourselves to be loved. To believe ourselves to be loved with an unconditional and unending love is to believe we are worthwhile, capable of living, and able to love. This confidence sets us free: free to live, free to love, free to be. With his faith in God's love, Jesus rejected slavery and accepted this freedom.

This same source of power and life is available to us. Our worth does not reside in any human power or person or achievement external to us. It is within us, given by the Creator of life. When we choose to trust our own worth, our sense of personal richness, and to base our actions on it, then we are free to live and to be helpful in empowering others to live also. Too many times we fail to make the connection that if we believe in Jesus, then it follows that we would believe in what Jesus believed about us: that we are unconditionally loved and forgiven, infinitely precious and useful.

Jesus rejected the three temptations, each of which would have located his identity and his power in something or someone outside himself, leaving him helpless and dependent. He chose instead to depend on the value he believed he had in himself, on the identity given him by God, as the source of his worth and his power. Such a choice is far more than a matter of intellectual assent. Choosing to believe in our worth as human beings means standing up for ourselves when we are scared and out of breath and vulnerable—at odds with the expectations of society or other people. It means acting out of our confidence in our own worth instead of reacting to the lures, taunts, or threats around us. By choosing to depend on his internal security, Jesus was free to live in the world in the most appropriate, effective, productive, and loving ways possible.

The wisdom of these ancient stories reveals one more amazing insight. It was only *after* Jesus had chosen his identity and found his worth in himself that he became truly powerful, productive, and able to help others. Matthew's first three chapters describe no activities on Jesus' part before affirming his identity. Then, as soon as he made his tough choices in the wilderness, Jesus became highly productive. In a few verses, he has chosen his twelve disciples and has begun teaching, preaching, and healing. The painful, personal choice of his authentic identity as a child of God put him in touch with the power and life of God within him. This allowed him to become a source of power and life to others, who are also the children of God.

So it is with our power and productivity. The more we choose to trust in ourselves and our basic worth as persons, the more effective and capable we become of functioning as human beings. Faith in God gives us faith in ourselves. We are who Jesus says we are. We grow in our ability to love and our competence to act in needed and responsible ways.

Responsibility is learned and chosen, just as is helplessness. But how is responsibility taught? That is one of the most frequent and fervent questions I hear from parents. What can I do to help my kids grow up to be responsible adults? According to the highly regarded psychiatrist William Glasser, in his book *Reality Therapy*, the most effective way to teach responsibility is by being responsible.[3]

---

[3] William Glasser, *Reality Therapy* (New York: Harper & Row, 1965), p. 17f. Copyright © 1965 by William Glasser, Inc.

Glasser illustrates his point with a story about dealing with his own children. One of his five-year-old son's greatest delights was to fill the big bathtub, put in his collection of water toys, and splash around happily. One evening, thinking it would be something his son would enjoy, Glasser filled the tub with water, put in the toys, and then called his son to come get in. Wanting to assert his independence, the boy said no. The father persisted in urging his son to get into the tub, but the boy repeated his refusal.

While this debate was going on, the boy's older sister came through, saw the tub full of water, zipped off her clothes, and jumped in. Immediately, of course, the son wanted to get in also. But this time it was the father who said no. He explained that the boy had had his chance and refused it. Now he must be bathed in the small bathtub and go on to bed.

Glasser undressed his son, put him into the small tub, and washed him. All the while the boy was having a tantrum: screaming, crying, kicking. The father said nothing. He simply continued to go about getting the boy ready for bed. Even when he was put to bed, the boy continued to scream and cry—and the father remained silent.

When the boy finally understood his protests were doing no good, he became quiet. Then the father went back into the bedroom, knelt down beside his son's bed, and said, "Just remember: Never say no when you mean yes."

That story had a tremendous impact on my life when I read it twenty-five years ago. I had young children then and realized that, in a similar situation, I would probably want to avoid the angry hassle. I probably would have given in to the boy's tantrum and said, "OK, this time you can go ahead and get into the big tub. But after this remember: Don't say no when you mean yes." But what he would have remembered is that by throwing a tantrum, he managed to get what he wanted. Without the slightest intention of doing so, I would

have taught him that. I would have taught him the effectiveness of irresponsible behavior. Giving in to his tantrum would
have been irresponsible behavior on my part, and that's what
Glasser means by saying that we teach responsibility by being
responsible. Glasser summarizes his point: "Parents who are
willing to suffer the pain of the child's intense anger by firmly
holding him to the responsible course are teaching him a
lesson that will help him all his life."[4]

How can responsibility be taught? A biblical response
with contemporary clarity is found in the fifth chapter of the
Gospel according to John. It gives us a dramatic example of
how the shift from a victim mentality to one of responsibility
completely changed a person's life. The chapter begins with
Jesus walking among the "multitudes of invalids, blind, lame,
paralyzed" who lay around a pool in Jerusalem called Bethzatha
(rendered in some translations as Bethesda, from which the
famous hospital in Maryland gets its name). The pool probably
was fed by an underground spring. The sick people were there
because of a local superstition that the first person into the
pool after the waters were "troubled," that is, began to
bubble, would be healed. Jesus came to a man who had been
there for thirty-eight years; and, even though he knew the man
had been there for a long time, Jesus asked him what appears
on the surface to be an insensitive and even insulting question,
"Do you want to be healed?"

We might have expected the man to say, "Of course!
Why do you think I've been here so long?" But how the man
did in fact respond reveals the wisdom of Jesus' question.
"Sir, I have no man to put me into the pool when the water is
troubled, and while I am going, another steps down before
me." These words reflect how he saw himself and what he felt
about himself: he was a victim. That self-image was the dominating reality of his life, and it left him so full of self-pity and

---

[4] Ibid, p. 18.

the need to explain his lifetime of inactivity and misfortune that he couldn't engage in an honest conversation. He probably didn't even hear the question. He had resigned himself to be sick, helpless, hopeless, and defensive for the rest of his life.

Jesus was not there to debate the merits of the super-stition or who was to blame for the man's painful and unpro-ductive life, either of which would have fueled an argument that could drag on for days and days without the possibility of any satisfactory conclusion. And during the argument the man would have continued to be a helpless invalid. Jesus was not there to be a part of a debate but to work for human wholeness. So, instead of getting caught up in the invalid's distracting excuses, Jesus went immediately to the heart of the issue. Believing the man had within him what he needed to move from being a cripple to being a responsible and func-tioning human being, Jesus challenged him to take responsi-bility for his own life. To the man who had been lying in a state of helpless despair for thirty-eight years, Jesus said: "Rise, take up your pallet, and walk."

Perhaps no one had ever spoken to him like that before. Whatever the reason, the man immediately responded to Jesus' challenge. As soon as he accepted responsibility for his condition, he had a new life: "And at once the man was healed, and he took up his pallet and walked" (John 5:9).

In a pattern reminiscent of Peter's experience of walking on the water, this man was willing to picture himself doing something he had never done before and, up to that moment, had never believed he could. Then, having dared to to see himself in this new and responsible light, he dared to act on that new picture. He got himself up and began walking.

How is responsibility taught and learned? One of the biggest features that emerges from all we have examined is that people learn responsibility by being allowed to experience the consequences of their own decisions and their own behavior. This was true of Glasser's son and of the man whose life was changed beside the pool at Bethzatha.

I recently saw one of my daughters treating her two-and-a-half-year-old son in this way, and I was proud and pleased with her. We were taking a walk through a small park behind their home. The path on which we were walking was plenty wide enough for all of us, but my grandson kept getting off into the thorny underbrush on both sides of the path. My daughter cautioned her son several times to stay on the path, but he seemed determined to do it his way. Finally, calmly but firmly, his mother told him that if he got off the path one more time, we'd have to go home. Immediately the boy jumped into the underbrush. Without any words or threats or even any angry gestures, Nancy picked up her crying, protesting son and carried him home. My grandson was given an opportunity to experience the consequences of his own choices and behavior.

One of the beauties of this understanding, especially to those of who didn't know about it when we were parenting, is that there's no need for anger, no need to attack the child and live in an atmosphere of cold hostility until the outward vestiges of the crisis finally wear away. The inward bruises only deepen and become more crippling and painful. There is still some pain, of course, for both the parent and the child, but this is the necessary and inevitable pain associated with growth. It is the pain that Glasser referred to as necessary suffering. It is an example of what Scott Peck had in mind in his frequent insistence that the unwillingness to experience necessary suffering is the basic cause for most mental illness.

Without rancor or recrimination, my grandson was allowed to experience what it is like to accept responsibility for his own decisions and his own behavior. He was permitted to be a part of the process of learning to be responsible. As he grows through adolesence and into adulthood, he will be better able to acknowledge his mistakes and better prepared to take whatever action is necessary to deal with them.

Dr. Jane Nelsen has a name for what happens more often in American families. She calls it the "Bawl Out–Bail Out" system. It is common for parents to bawl out their kids for failing to do something they'd been told time and time again they should do, such as putting away their bikes so they won't be stolen. In this tirade the kids get accused of being lazy, irresponsible, selfish, and spoiled. If a bike ever is stolen, those parents say, "Well, I hope you've learned your lesson. So now we'll go to town and buy a new bike,. This time, take care of it!" What the kids actually learn from the experience is that if they endure the rants and raves, the demeaning and humiliating remarks, someone else will bail them out of the situation. They learn helplessness rather than responsibility.

The importance of learning to choose responsibility over helplessness can hardly be exaggerated. Choosing to be responsible, and allowing others the opportunity to make that choice also, is the point about which there is virtual unanimity among all the leading spokespersons in the behavioral sciences. John Bradshaw, for example, sees this as a central part of moving beyond shame-based living to greater personal health.

> Aside from acts of God, you are responsible for what happens in your world. I suggested earlier that neuroses and character disorders are dis-orders of responsibility. Learning to be respons-ible and to allow others that privilege is to live in reality. Ask yourself, "What choices have I made that resulted in this situation? What decisions can I now make to change it?" Also remember that respect for others means letting them live their

own lives, suffer their own pains and solve their
own problems.[5]

Which friends are truly friends? Which counselors
actually help us to become better able to live? Which doctors
are effective healers? Which business managers fulfill the
directive to "help people to win?" Those whose self-esteem is
within them, who trust and build on the foundation of their
worth as persons, who take responsibility for their own lives.
Effective, capable people are those who have been out in the
loneliness and dangers of their own personal wildernesses
and there chose to trust in their worth as human beings. Such
people have high self-esteem and are able to take responsibility for their own lives.

Martin Luther had a special way of handling stress. The
man who set off the whole Protestant Reformation by challenging the authority of hierarchical decrees and insisting
that "salvation is by faith alone" practiced exactly that. In
moments of personal crisis, he would say to himself, "I have
been baptized." In his times of adversity he found security in
the faith that he was accepted and loved. He chose to accept
that identity as his source of worth and power and hope. His
foundation was within him.

---

[5] John Bradshaw, *Healing the Shame That Binds You* (Deerfield
Beach, FL: Heath Communications, 1988), p. 200.

CHAPTER SEVEN

Self-Esteem
and Community

Even though we must take full personal responsibility for our own self-esteem as adults, we cannot do that without the assistance of others. Does that sound contradictory? It is another of life's beautiful but perplexing paradoxes. To be most fully alive as our own authentic and unique selves, we need to be a part of a community. But what kind of community? What do we need from others, and they from us? What is the healthiest and most creative way for people to live together in community?

Many people have spent most of their lives believing that God commands us to be our brothers' keepers. They are amazed to learn that there is absolutely no scriptural basis for that assumption. According to the Bible, that idea actually came from a lying murderer. God never even speaks the words "brother's keeper." In fact, based on the scriptures as a whole, being our brothers' keepers is just the opposite of what God wants from us. The consistent message of the will of God as revealed in Jesus Christ is that we are called to be our brothers' and sisters' brothers and sisters.

The mistaken notion that we are to be our brothers' keepers arises from a story in the fourth chapter of the book of Genesis. There we are introduced to Cain and Abel, the sons of Adam and Eve. "Now Abel was a keeper of sheep"—notice that *keeper* is the word used to describe Abel's relation to the sheep—"and Cain a tiller of the ground" (Genesis 4:2b). In the course of time, both Cain and Abel brought an offering to the Lord. For reasons that are never explained, God found the offering of Abel to be acceptable, but Cain's was not. Cain, understandably, was angry; and God lectured him about getting control of himself.

Then Cain invited Abel out into the field. Unfortunately, that was the last invitation Abel ever received or accepted. As soon as they got out into the field, Cain killed his brother. God immediately asked Cain: "Where is Abel your brother?" And Cain responded: "I do not know; am I my brother's keeper?" (Genesis 4:9).

Cain, the murderer, is the one who coined the phrase "brother's keeper." He introduced the term as an attempt to cover his guilt. He's like a boy who, without permission, has been playing with his older brother's football. The ball rolls out into the street, where a truck runs over and destroys it. That night the older brother asks, "Have you seen my football?" The guilty brother replies, "Heck no! Am I supposed to keep track of your stuff?"

The older brother never suggested that the younger boy was supposed to look out for his football, and God never suggested to Cain that he was supposed to be his brother's keeper. In both cases what we hear from the guilty brothers is a purposely exaggerated overstatement by which they are attempting to construct an illusion of innocence.

The fact that Abel is introduced as a "keeper of sheep" is significant. Animals in captivity need keepers—to feed them, protect them, direct where they are to go, decide when their usefulness has ended. Doing that to human beings is demeaning and dehumanizing. It distorts their integrity as human beings and assaults their sense of worth.

The consistent direction of the biblical stories indicates that God wants all people to be loving, caring, accepting, forgiving, respecting, nurturing brothers and sisters to all the rest of humanity—to all their brothers and sisters. Mother Teresa has captivated the world's attention with her insistence that every starving, dying derelict on the streets of Calcutta, or anywhere else in the world, deserves loving treatment as a child of God, regardless of what his or her religious or racial heritage may be. She does not try to convert those to whom she gives her love and compassion. She does not see herself as the keeper of their bodies or their souls. She cares for them that they may experience what she believes to be the truth: that they are loved and precious human beings, deserving to be treated with dignity and respect. She's been quoted as saying that her goal is for each of those dying human beings, at least once before death, to hear and experience the reality that he or she is loved.

At the center of the Christian faith is the conviction of God's love for all people. For Christians this conviction is affirmed in the person of Jesus Christ, in whom the reality of God's love becomes human, personal, touchable. For Christians the love of God is far more than a theological or philosophical proposition. In Jesus Christ that love "became flesh and dwelt among us" (John 1:14). And the church, referred to in scripture as the "body of Christ," is called by God to be the human community in which that love continues to be a personal, touchable, flesh-and-blood reality.

The Westminster Confession of Faith, written over a period of many years in seventeenth-century England, has long been the single most influential statement of faith within what is called the "Reformed Tradition." When we read in that ancient and revered document that "there is no ordinary possibility of salvation outside the church," we need to understand that its writers were not attempting to limit people's access to salvation. They were affirming that, so far as they could understand the way God works (and they used the word *ordinary* to acknowledge that their understanding of how God works *was* limited), no one could come to a saving knowledge that he or she is loved without experiencing that love within a nurturing human community. The Westminster Divines put those words together more than 300 years ago. Yet those words are amazingly similar—and their ideas even more so— to what we read today in a nonreligious context in the writings of M. Scott Peck: "In and through community lies the salvation of the world. . . . Nothing is more important."[1]

Scott Peck became rich and famous as a result of *The Road Less Traveled*, a book on personal growth. In another book, *A Different Drum*, this advocate of the discipline and commitment necessary for individual growth tells us that nothing is more important than the creation of community. Personal growth cannot be accomplished by a person on his or her own. It depends on our involvement and participation in a nurturing community. Learning to love ourselves is inescapably linked with being part of a supportive community.

Peck acknowledges the unfortunate circumstance that hardly any of us know what we're talking about when we speak of community because "most of us have never had an experience of true community." As he says, it is impossible to communicate an understanding of community to those who have never experienced it, but for the purposes of discussion, he does provide us with a descriptive definition.

> . . . we must restrict [the meaning of the word *community*] to a group of individuals who have learned how to communicate honestly with each

---

[1] M. Scott Peck, *A Different Drum* (New York: Simon & Schuster, 1987), p. 17. Copyright © 1987 by M. Scott Peck, M.D., P.C. Reprinted by permission of Simon & Schuster.

> other, whose relationships go deeper than their masks of composure, and who have developed some significant commitment to "rejoice together, mourn together," and to "delight in each other, make others' conditions our own."[2]

As I pondered this definition, wondering where such a community really exists, I remembered my experiences in waiting rooms outside hospital intensive care units. Many a time I've seen a remarkable community come into existence in such a setting. People gather in these waiting rooms because someone dear to them is in a life-threatening situation. So the conversations among them tend to be far more honest, far less superficially social, than what we usually find elsewhere.

As those people wait together for many long hours, day after day, they learn to know each other very well—and at a level much deeper than most of their relationships beyond that room. Sorrows and fears and hopes are expressed and received and understood. In the depth of the bond that develops among them, they learn to care profoundly. When a doctor comes in with a report for one family, all the others in that room share the anticipation and yearning of that announcement. In Peck's words, they "rejoice together, mourn together, delight in each other, and make others' conditions their own." Real community!

We're all in life's waiting room together.

The words Peck uses to define *community* can also be used to describe the properly functioning, supportive, nurturing family that helps develop self-esteem and healthy human beings. Our need for a nurturing, supporting group does not end when we move out of childhood and adolescence into our adult years. The right kind of family (community)

---

[2] Ibid, p. 59.

continues to be essential for our growth as persons, as well as being essential for the creation of a peaceful and productive world. Our need to be in a family-like community never ends. Let me detail this need by means of a brief and slightly simplistic description of the developmental movement of a person through adolescence into adulthood.

Children in their early years find a healthy strength and confidence in being able to identify with their parents: "I'm Daddy's boy," or "I'm Mommy's girl." The world is big and frightening. Small and dependent children need someone bigger and stronger in whom to find a sense of worth and protection. Being in a family plays a crucial part in their development.

When the children move into their adolescent years, however, it is important for them to be able to let go of that dependency, to move out on their own, to become persons who have there own identity, no longer having to cling to their parents for protection or confidence. This process of individuation is absolutely essential for the young people but a very painful process for the parents. (Haim Ginott once said that parents are the anvils on whom children beat out their lives.) To establish their individual identities and their ability to stand on their own, young people must demonstrate their separateness from all adults, but especially from those adults on whom they were previously dependent for their identities: their parents.

Most parents make it difficult for their children to establish this separation. Parents like the stroking to their egos that comes from having the identification and adoration of their kids. Most parents are equally intense in their dislike for seeing themselves and everything they hold dear being questioned and repudiated by their own gangly and ungrateful offspring. But by making it difficult for their kids to accomplish the needed separation, parents unwittingly push their kids farther and farther away, forcing them to be all the more rebellious and outrageous to make the point that their lives are indeed their own.

Unfortunately, sometimes the parents win this painful struggle. Through the use of guilt and bribes and intimidation they may keep their kids from accomplishing the necessary work of adolescence. Such kids meekly and submissively give up their efforts to move out and establish their own identities. They continue unthinking support to mom and dad's values and world views. These children become adults who are still mommy's girl and daddy's boy, or daddy's girl and mommy's boy. The parents may swell with pride that they have such considerate and accommodating children, not aware how those young lives are being stifled and stunted. Such young-sters have great difficulty ever being persons on their own, which may well be an even worse fate than that of their peers who go through giant and destructive rebellions.

Under the best possible circumstances, parents under-stand their children's need to break away and establish their own identities. These parents support that growth, even though it always involves them in some pain. Once adoles-cents have been able to experience themselves as separate and distinct, recognizing themselves as having identities and capabilities of their own, they are able to return to a relation-ship with their parents. They return no longer as submissive children but as adult human beings relating to other adult human beings with whom they share the precious bonds of a common history, many years of mutual experiences, much acceptance, understanding, growth, and love.

A wise commentator once said that the goal of parents is to love their children so much that their children no longer need them. What could be more satisfying to parents than to see their children become responsible adults, able to care for themselves and to make their own decisions, capable of living fulfilling and productive lives? If there *is* anything more satis-fying, then surely it is the experience of having those adult children choose to return and spend time with their parents—not because they must or are coerced into doing so, but because they enjoy the mutual respect and appreciation they are able to share with their parents as human beings.

Children need the support of their families to make friends, to leave home, to find their own lives and their own values—even if that means defying some of the values and dreams of the family. Without the support of the family, it is difficult and unbelievably painful for young people to accomplish this essential step in their growth.

For the same reasons, the need for a nurturing, supportive community never ends. Throughout our lives we continue to need a "family" to understand and accept us, a community that encourages us and gives us persmission to go out and be persons on our own, even if sometimes that means taking a stand that sets us apart from the prevailing stance of the community. Actually, it is crucially important for a healthy community that there be some "rebels," some innovative thinkers who push against the posture and policy of the Establishment. Otherwise there will be no growth for the community, or the country—only a "stuckness" in an old and degenerative rut.

We need to feel safe about being the unique persons we are without losing our sense of being loved. This happens when we can express our differences and still find acceptance on the part of our community, whether other members agree with us or not. We simply cannot function all on our own. We never become so mature, so grown up, so independent, that we no longer need the nurturing of a community. Indeed it is the nurturing of the community that provides us with the necessary foundation for continuing to grow in our personal maturity and independence.

There is "no ordinary possibility of salvation" outside the community because we cannot accept ourselves until we have experienced the reality of acceptance from outside ourselves. To learn how to accept what has always been unacceptable in our own minds and emotions, we need to experience being accepted. Therapists are sometimes said to be paid friends, necessary because we often don't know how to be friends to each other. This is precisely why psychotherapy and experiences in a Christian community have been crucial for so many of us. At their best, both allow us to experience understanding and acceptance. We cannot forgive ourselves until we have experienced the reality of forgiveness from others.

We also need to be a part of offering nurturance and acceptance and encouragement and forgiveness to others who are involved in their processes of going out and coming back. This process is an essential part of growth in all our lives. We are nurtured, loved, and encouraged; we venture out to become independent, thoughtful, responsible persons. And we return to be nurturing and nurtured, accepting and accepted, understanding and understood, forgiving and forgiven. This going out and coming back is the process of living and growing we go through as toddlers learning to walk, as children on the first day of school, as teens finding our peer groups, and as adults exploring our worlds and our unique selves.

This is a paradox and must be understood as such. Is it healthier to be "your own person," self-determined, standing on your own convictions and by your own strength, separate and free from the influences and constraints of others? Or is it more desirable to be a member of a family or community group, giving support to and receiving it from others? For wholeness, it cannot be one or the other. Both are necessary for our personal growth and the journey toward healthier self-esteem.

Dr. Mary Mallory, a professsor of psychology at California State University, Fresno, offers this insight:

> No one can give self-esteem to anyone else. We can
> provide a supportive environment for personal
> growth, opportunities for successful experiences
> in goal-directed behavior, and productive roles for
> all citizens.[3]

Understanding that we cannot give self-esteem to each other takes a lot of pressure off us. It also releases the people on whom we, with nothing but the best of intentions, might try to impose our wonderful "cures." The nature of community thus excludes seeking to impose what we think is "best" for others. Such coercion detracts from their self-respect and responsibility as human beings. That's acting as if we are their keepers.

This concept of community does imply, however, that we have a responsibility to family members, the people with whom we work and study, others in our neighborhoods and our country, and ultimately, all the other human beings with whom we share this planet. We are responsible for creating nurturing and affirming environments in all the communities of which we are a part. Such communities offer people the best possible opportunity to make positive decisions about themselves.

The effects of such communities are remarkable, as research by the internationally known psychologist and author of *Parent Effectiveness Training,* Thomas Gordon, shows.

> Managers who develop democratic relationships
> (use a participative management style) with their
> work groups develop workers with higher produc-
> tivity, high morale, lower turnover, fewer griev-
> ances, less absenteeism. In addition, they feel

---

[3] *Toward a State of Esteem,* California Task Force to Promote Self-Esteem, and Personal and Social Responsibility (Sacramento, CA: California State Department of Education, 1990), p. 8.

> better about themselves, like to go to work, have
> more self-esteem and self-confidence, less sense
> of powerlessness. . . .
>
> Teachers who manage their classrooms more
> democratically have fewer discipline problems
> and foster better study habits and high scholastic
> achievement. . . .
>
> Parents who govern their families democratically,
> who refrain from using power to control family
> members in making family rules, who try to facili-
> tate all family members getting their needs met—
> such parents produce youngsters who are healthier
> emotionally as well as physically and who function
> more effectively in many different ways.[4]

At a time when most people in the United States express
serious reservations about the relevance and importance of
the church, according to how they vote with their feet, the
evidence is more compelling than ever that what the church
could offer is absolutely essential. Ideally, it could be a
nurturing, affirming, supportive, loving, accepting, forgiving
human community that points beyond itself to a truly unconditional and enduring love. As Peck says, nothing matters
more.

Many of us can remember times when the church community was there for us, accepting and supporting and standing with us when we were not able to stand by ourselves.
These are the times when the church fulfills its God-given
mandate. As explained by Dr. D. T. Niles of Ceylon, recognized
throughout Christendom as this century's leading authority
on evangelism, "To invite a person to Christ is to invite that
person into a loving family."[5]

---

[4] Thomas Gordon, in an unfinished manuscript made available to
the author in 1989.
[5] D. T. Niles, in an address given at the Princeton Theological
Seminary Sesquicentennial in April 1962.

Typically, the church best handles its role as a loving family in times of physical or medical crises, or when there is a death. I have often witnessed a congregation ministering in such situations with magnificent courage and compassion, as an instrument of life. Most churches find it more difficult to play that same role when the issue is an offense against some moral standard. Yet the Midwestern church that accepted and supported Dave's unwed mother and later Dave himself is evidence that a nurturing role is possible even under difficult circumstances.

In his classic *Les Miserables*, Victor Hugo preserved a dramatic example of the church at its finest: making Christ's mercy real for an outsider in desperate need. A bishop provided food and shelter for a vagrant, Jean Valjean. Valjean was later apprehended by the police, who found him with treasures he'd stolen from the bishop's house. When the police brought Valjean back to the bishop, the bishop brought out his silver candlesticks, saying Valjean had forgotten to take that part of his gift. Valjean later acknowledged that the bishop's acceptance and forgiveness had changed his entire life, saying he began to believe in himself because he'd been treated better than he deserved. That is acceptance. It exemplifies an experience of the gospel of grace. Even when we commit deeds that are unworthy, we can be made worthy by God's love. To believe we are loved is to be made worthy by that love. To create and convey such experiences is the responsibility of the community of the church, serving as the body of Christ.

By its own statement of faith, the church has greater resources than any other group for becoming this kind of community. By definition, followers of Christ are ones who acknowledge that they've been treated better than they deserve. Christ bids those followers to love as he has loved them: to extend sympathy to people who expect judgment, generosity to those who expect retribution, new opportunities and hope to the defeated and hopeless.

Biblical accounts describe this as precisely what people in Galilee experienced from Jesus. He not only said to them, "Come to me all of you who labor and are heavy laden and I will give you rest" (Matthew 11:28), he delivered on his promise. He fed the hungry, healed the sick and lame, forgave the guilty, accepted the outcasts, gave his friendship to those who had no friends. He offered community to those who had none, and his primary support came from those who had been rejected by society. He challenged the authenticity of the existing religious community, and his primary opposition was from religious leaders who wanted to maintain the illusion of their spiritual superiority.

Why has experiencing the "good news" of the gospel been such a rare happening? Why do we so often come away from our experiences in the church feeling worse, like reprehensible sinners, like the worst of the worst, like phonies, fearing no one there would have anything to do with us if they really knew who we are and what we have done? Why don't we get that wonderful renewal of feeling that "We're all in this thing together"?

Because we are still captive to precisely the same fear that the gospel is designed to combat. To some extent or another, worse on some days and better on others, we fear that we do not matter. To take care of this incessant fear, we look for ways of living that allow us to compete in "proving" that our existence is significant. For some, this involves showing that they matter more than someone else. Some try to prove their worth with money. Some with fame. Some with pedigree or race or education or friends or beauty or athletic achievements. And some seek to prove that they matter through religion, by showing that they are more devout, more learned, more correct, more righteous.

The reality behind any sanctimonious front is fear: the fear of insignificance. The rest of the world sees that sometimes intimidating front for what it is: a feigned superiority.

Meanwhile the community (or the congregation that was to build on the message that "We're all in this thing together") becomes a vicious arena of comparisons, judgments, proofs, put-downs, and banishment.

For example, the church hierarachy "silenced" Matthew Fox, the Roman Catholic priest we quoted earlier, for his pioneering work in critiquing the historical basis for the doctrine of original sin. They did not want him advancing views that threatened their orthodoxy. Fox remarked at the time that the church seemed to him like a dysfunctional family.

Surely Peck is right that nothing matters more than creating nurturing and supportive communities whose acceptance and encouragement and caring make it possible for us to experience ourselves as persons of worth. In such communities we are able to make new and more positive decisions about our self-esteem, to be reborn. We can discover a new world and a new life for ourselves within it. It is the essence of the church to be that new community. Yet, far too often, the church proves to be an extension of the dysfunctional families from which we have come.

So the mainline churches today are in a state of decline, both in numbers and in public respect. At the same time we're witnessing an amazing growth of what are called Twelve-Step programs: communities modeled on Alcoholics Anonymous. Twelve-Step programs exist for many groups: the spouses of alcoholics, the children of alcoholics, compulsive gamblers, overeaters, those suffering from suicides in their families, drug abusers, the families of drug abusers, people reared in fundamentalist churches, ex-clergy, ex-prostitutes, and so forth.

Twelve-Step programs succeed by offering what people need most: a nurturing, accepting, supportive community. These programs are more like what the church is intended to be than are most churches. People who enter a Twelve-Step program do so acknowledging their needs. In both philosophy and structure, the programs are designed to discourage any efforts to look better than someone else. People who become members do so with the humbling acknowledgment that "I have a problem that has become uncontrollable in my life." Thus the ideal for the church, the idea that "We're all in this thing together," is given actual, personal expression.

In my experience, these programs do strive for absolute acceptance. In the community they provide, the goal is to allow every participant to feel worthy and welcome. At the same time, no one is mollycoddled and told "That's OK. Just do the best you can." What evolves are communities of people who have found understanding and acceptance and who have understanding and acceptance to share with others. This allows all of them to grow in their sense of worth, their ability to handle their problems, and their ability to live.

There are people who have not found their needs met in the Twelve-Step programs of which they became a part. These programs are no more free from the perils of human fearfulness than any other part of our society, but they do have the enormous advantage of acknowledging their fearfulness in both their structure and in their dealings with each other.

Alongside the increasing popularity of the Twelve-Step programs, many people are registering their feelings of having been abandoned by their churches. Dissappointed and hurt with the churches' failures to provide what they are charged to give, and what we need so desperately, many respond by reciprocating: abandoning the church. Unfortunately, those who leave sometimes carry with them their unresolved feelings of hurt and outrage. They may remain needy and needing, still unsure and doubting that there is any hope. In leaving they abandon, for themselves and for the world, what we all need most: a human community of love and acceptance that is able to put us in contact with a love and acceptance that are truly unconditional and eternal. In such a community there is hope. Nothing matters more.

Few places outside the Bible itself have I found this message articulated with more compelling and personal relevance than in the words of the Italian playwright Ugo Betti. In his play *The Burnt Flower-Bed,* one of his characters says,

> "That's what's needed, don't you see. *That!* Nothing else matters half so much. To reassure one another. To answer each other. Perhaps only you can listen to me and not laugh. Everyone has, inside himself ... a very great, very important character! ... Every man must be persuaded—even if he's in rags— that he's immensely, immensely important! Everyone must respect him; and make him respect himself too. They must listen to him attentively. Don't stand on top of him, don't stand in his light. But look at him with deference. Give him great, great hopes, he needs them ... especially if he's young. Spoil him! Yes, make him grow proud."[6]

Betti sounds more like an advocate of the self-esteem movement than a playwright.

Christianity does not call us to be our brother's keeper. It calls us to be brothers and sisters to our brothers and sisters. We can be a family, a community, in which all people can discover themselves to be "immensely, immensely important!" Nothing else matters half so much.

---

[6] Ugo Betti, *Three Plays* (New York: Grove Press, 1958), p. 151.

CHAPTER EIGHT

What Can I Do To Help?

"What can I do to help?" How often have you heard that? How often have you asked it? Something within us feels a longing (for some of us, it's close to being a compulsion) to be of help. But how: What's needed?

Being an effective helper has a lot to do with self-esteem. This chapter examines several examples. The first involves Mary and Martha, sisters who both loved Jesus, though they had radically different ways of expressing their love. One time Jesus went to their house for a visit, and these differences became obvious—and revealing.

Martha immediately went into the kitchen and threw herself into the task of preparing a meal that would be appropriate for one whom she admired and liked very much. She kept herself busy serving, making sure Jesus lacked for nothing. Mary, however, simply sat at Jesus' feet, absorbing every word, every meaning, every living vibration Jesus had to share. After a while, and quite understandably, Martha got upset with Mary's sitting there in the living room enjoying Jesus while she, Martha, was stuck with the serving. So Martha went to Jesus (not to Mary) and asked him to instruct Mary to get up and give her a hand with the work.

Jesus cared a lot about both sisters, and he understood them well. He didn't tell Mary to stop doing what she was doing and to start doing what Martha wanted her to do. Nor did he in any way reprove Martha for what she was doing—nor even for wanting Mary to help her do it. The chances are that Martha was doing the best she knew to do. Her busyness was her way of expressing love, a love for which Jesus was grateful. You can almost feel the gentleness and caring in the way he spoke her name: "Martha, Martha, you are anxious and troubled about many things; one thing is needful. Mary has chosen the good portion, which shall not be taken from her" (Luke 10:41, 42).

I'm glad Jesus was gentle and accepting with Martha because I identify with her—a lot. Martha's busyness was a covering for low self-esteem, as it is with many of us. For instance, I often find myself anxious and troubled about many things; and, in a situation of high importance, it seems natural for me to begin serving. I think this indicates I have more confidence in what I do than in who I am. It's not strange that I should be this way. Since childhood I've been praised and appreciated for my achievements—for what I've done—not for who I am. So when I want to make a good impression or express the depths of my caring, I feel I have to do something. Seeing this in myself lets me know some fear still exists deep within me as it did in Martha—that who I am is not enough.

Mary, on the other hand, seemed quite content just to sit there, giving Jesus her full attention. Somehow, she believed that she was enough, even though she was doing nothing beyond being there, listening and caring.

In our defensiveness, some of us "doers" may say, "Well, if somebody hadn't been doing what Martha was doing, nobody would have been eating." This may be true. I do not discount the importance or worth of what Martha was doing; neither did Jesus. But we need to look at it. What Jesus said was that one thing was needful. What was it?

Biblical scholars offer a wide variety of speculations as to what Jesus meant. From my perspective on this passage, and on the gospel as a whole, I think the one needful thing was the ability to enter into an experience of love—love given and love received—in which the deepest possible expression is giving attention. This difference in their ability to love is what I see as the crucial difference between Mary and Martha in this story.

Defining something so multidimensional as love limits and, therefore, distorts it. Although this leaves me skeptical of *any* definition of love, I find Scott Peck's definition thoughtful and intriguing. He says love is: "The will to extend one's self for the purpose of nurturing one's own or another's spiritual growth."[1]

The word *will* indicates that before love is an emotion, it is a decision: a choice of will. That choice is to "extend one's self," that is, to go beyond our comfort zone. Rather than staying in the security of where we've always been, we choose to risk moving out past the point where we feel safe. The purpose of this action is growth, spiritual growth (which to Peck is the same as human growth).

This definition fits equally well when we're talking about loving ourselves or when we're talking about loving someone else. This understanding of love is completely consistent with Jesus' command to love others in the same way we love ourselves. It also provides revealing insights into Mary and Martha. Mary made a choice to focus her time and attention

---

[1] M. Scott Peck, *The Road Less Traveled* (New York: Simon & Schuster, 1978), p. 81. Copyright © 1978 by M. Scott Peck, M.D., P.C. Reprinted by permission of Simon & Schuster.

on Jesus. Martha also chose to do what she was doing, but she was exerting rather than extending herself. She hadn't made a new decision in this moment, taking into consideration the unique needs and opportunities of this particular situation. Martha was doing what she'd always done, what she'd always felt comfortable doing: expressing her love through acts of service.

Mary, on the other hand, did extend herself. She dared to risk her sister's displeasure and the possibility that Jesus might think of her as lazy and unproductive. She extended herself for the sake of her spiritual growth: growth in her confidence in being herself and growth in her knowledge, her understanding, her relationship with Jesus.

While Mary chose to put herself in a position where she could experience growth, Martha stayed where she'd always been, doing what she'd always done. Maybe "doing" was still the best she could manage at that point in her life. Martha not only stayed stuck, her anxious doing separated her from Jesus and her sister. Jesus didn't criticize Martha. He did let her know that Mary had found the "good portion," and he wasn't going to take that away.

One more aspect seems very exciting to me. Not only was Mary loving herself by choosing to center her attention on Jesus, she was also loving Jesus in the fullest way possible. Listening, according to Peck, is the most important work of love.

> The principal form that the work of love takes is attention. When we love another we give him or her our attention. . . . By far the most common and important way in which we can exercise our attention is by listening.[2]

---

[2] Ibid, p. 120.

This is, for me, an outstanding example of how insights from modern psychology can bring clarity and depth to the ancient stories from the Bible. It's not that psychology adds any truth to the stories, but it does allow us to comprehend and appreciate their truth in ways that might not otherwise be available to us. The interaction between theology and psychology produces a relationship of mutual enlightenment and vitality.

The Mary and Martha story had such an impact on me that, for a while, it seemed to me that being was everything and doing was nothing. The more I paid attention to the story and to life, however, I realized that this isn't so. Doing is very important; but it is crucial for us to understand that effective doing flows forth from being, not the other way around.

For example, once I knew a teenage girl who, for a variety of reasons, was plagued with an enormously low self-esteem. Other kids in her church fellowship group were remarkably caring and understanding of her. One year, driven by her desire to be liked, she spent the week before Christmas baking cookies. Every night after baking, she'd deliver a box of fresh, warm cookies to the front door of each of the other kids in the group. As she stood there at the door, with a big smile on her face and a box of hot cookies in her hands, her friends could sense there was a price to be paid for their gift, as surely as if she'd handed them a bill. She was waiting for their assurance that she was at least a little bit wonderful.

At some time or another, most all of us have felt similar discomfort when under pressure to express thanks in a way that would meet the needs of the person we were thanking. Instinctively, we recognize we cannot convince someone else that he or she is loved, no matter what we say or do. Each of us either chooses to believe we are loved, or we don't get it. We have to take responsibility for our own self-esteem and choose it for ourselves.

If this young lady had done exactly the same things she was doing, only with some confidence in her own worth, the situation there at the door would have been completely different—though a photograph would have revealed no difference at all. If, when she handed over the cookies, she had been operating out of an image of herself as a loved person, her smile would have been an external sign of her inner delight and not a thin disguise for the urgency of her need to be praised. If she'd had some sense of herslf as being loved and capable, her giving would have been an expression of her love, her pleasure in giving, her joy in being a part of the group. In that scenario, the recipients would have felt delighted and honored to receive her gift.

This story explains what I mean by saying that our doing needs to flow forth from our being. When the girl was doing—baking and giving—in order to be loved, it didn't work. It never does. We cannot prove that we are loved, nor can we earn love. But when we believe ourselves to be loved and capable people, then our doing becomes a natural and appropriate expression of who we are. And it is exquisitely satisfying for everyone.

This examination of doing and being deals with some of the most frequently asked questions about personal growth in general and self-esteem in particular: What do I need to do to get it? What should I do to raise my self-esteem? How do I go about giving healthy self-esteem to my kids or my mate or my friends? What can I do to help?

The first answer, always, is to take responsibility for your own self-esteem. This is not simply because no one else can take responsibility for anyone else's self-esteem, but also because our ability to assist others who are working on their self-esteem exists in direct proportion to the health of our own. Only those with a sense of being loving and capable can effectively assist others to think of themselves as loving and capable. The most important influence in developing the self-esteem of children, for example, is the self-esteem of the parents. Similarly, Dr. Arthur Combs, Distinguished Professor at Northern Colorado University, found through a long-term and extensive study that effective learning does not depend on how much the teacher knows or on any particular educational system. It depends on the self-esteem of the teachers.[3]

Teachers who feel positive about themselves are able to create a positive atmosphere in their classrooms, which allows the students to feel positive about their possibilities to learn. Teachers with high self-esteem are less rigid and controlling. They encourage students to use their own ingenuity, to devleop their own styles. Combs reported that one of the great tragedies of the U.S. educational system is that students' success pivots on the ability to come up with the right answer. As a result, students tend to stick with the "one right way" shown by the teacher or laid out in their textbooks. This effectively stifles creativity, inventiveness, and imagination. To recover these crucial qualities, Combs advocates creating a system that encourages mistakes. Most people (and schools) scoff at that idea. Only teachers (or anyone else) with high self-esteem are able to tolerate a process that encourages mistakes.

The second answer to the question "What can I do to help?" is to understand what people need and to deal with them on the basis of their needs. We helpers often confuse this with our needs to help. The two are not the same. For example, demanding a rigidly controlled classroom may be far more important in meeting the emotional needs of the teacher than in providing the most conducive possible environment for learning. This is not to say that the teacher's needs don't matter. They do, just as much as the students' needs for recognition of their individuality and creativity.

---

[3] Arthur Combs, lecture at Self-Esteem Conference (San Jose, CA, 1988).

Neither set of needs benefits, ultimately, by being recognized and honored to the exclusion of the other.

Teachers who prize themselves and take care of their own needs in appropriate ways have the greatest capacity to be sensitive and helpful to the needs of their students. William Glasser, who writes about how quality is achieved in the classroom, compares this to the kind of work environment that promotes quality production:

> The more a manager focuses on the needs that are hardest to satisfy—belonging and power—and figures out how to manage in such a way that these needs are satisfied, the more successful he or she will be.[4]

Again and again, research has shown that caring is the single most important ingredient in both quality education and in providing the motivation to keep kids in school. So what can we do to show genuine caring? Peck says to give attention—by listening. Even listening, however, can become mechanical and impersonal. I've experienced people listening to me intently but in a way that was most unsatisfying. They were listening as they'd been trained to do, responding with some of the same words they'd heard from me, inserting my name frequently to show their interest. But I didn't experience myself being personally cared about or truly heard. I missed an underlying sense that the person who was listening to me was really there. That kind of listening is doing, not being.

Two phrases that I've found extremely helpful in explaining and talking about authentic caring come from Dr.

---

[4] William Glasser, *The Quality School* (New York: Harper & Row, 1990), p. 88.

Everett Shostrom.[5] *Manipulators* in relationships, says Shostrom, "do to" while *masters* in relationships are willing to "be with."

An example arises out of my own life. After finishing a workshop on this subject in Houston, I was on my way to the hill country in central Texas to give a weekend workshop. Along the way I would have just enough time to visit with my daughter, Dianne. All during the three-hour drive to be with her, I was thinking what I could do and say to make our time together as exciting and memorable as possible. Then, just as I was entering the outskirts of the city where Dianne lives, it struck me. My hours of planning had been an effort to "do to" Dianne: to create the climate, bring up the subjects, offer the suggestions, and maintain an attitude that would cause that visit to live in Dianne's memory forever. I wanted her to remember her father as thoughtful, caring, insightful, and wonderful.

After teaching about "being with" rather than "doing to," I had fallen into precisely the trap I was lobbying against. Having realized and acknowledged this, I spent a lot of my two hours with Dianne talking about it. As a result, I think we were able to "be with" each other in a very personal and satisfying way. And I, at least, have not forgotten that experience.

To be with a person means being willing to let ourselves be known as we are: scared, angry, unsure, lonely, hopeful, caring, happy, sad, or whatever combination of these we may feel at that particular moment. Being with also means being willing to let that other person be whoever he or she may be at the moment, without making any effort to talk that person out of a mood or way of thinking that displeases or frightens us.

---

[5] Everett Shostrom, *From Manipulator to Master* (New York: Bantam, 1983), p.13.

Being with means letting go of any effort to control other people, or the situation, or the outcome of the conversation, or our own image. It is something we seldom experience. Tragically, few people have enough self-esteem to believe they can survive such an interaction. Out of the fear that we are not enough, we are nearly always controlling, manipulating, doing to—and we are nearly always being controlled, manipulated, and done to.

Henri Nouwen, a Roman Catholic priest/author/theologian/psychologist, has done a marvelous job of describing what it means to be with another person:

> Still, when we honestly ask ourselves which persons in our lives mean the most to us, we often find that it is those who, instead of giving much advice, solutions, or cures, have chosen rather to share our pain and touch our wounds with a gentle and tender hand. The friend who can be silent with us in a moment of despair or confusion, who can stay with us in an hour of grief and berevement, who can tolerate not-knowing, not-curing, not-healing and face with us the reality of our powerlessness, that is the friend who cares.
>
> You might remember moments in which you were called to be with a friend who had lost a wife or husband, child or parent. What can you say, do, or propose at such a moment? There is a strong inclination to say, "Don't cry; the one you loved is in the hands of God." "Don't be sad because there are so many good things left worth living for." But are we ready to really experience our powerlessness in the face of death and say: "I do not understand. I do not know what to do but I am here with you." Are we willing to not run away from the pain, to not get busy when there is nothing to do and instead stand rather in the face of death together with those who grieve?

> rather in the face of death together with those who grieve?
>
> The friend who cares makes it clear that whatever happens in the external world, being present to each other is what really matters.[6]

A few paragraphs later, Nouwen sums it up in one masterful sentence: "Therefore, to care means first of all to be present to each other."[7] This, rather than giving in to our own need to do something, is the finest answer I know to the question "What can I do to help?" Being present to someone is the expression of a person who has taken responsibility for his or her own self-esteem. Only people with a healthy sense of self-esteem are able to let go of the anxious need to control or to prove themselves. By letting go, they are able to be present to others vulnerably and authentically.

Being with people also affirms our confidence in them. It affirms our acceptance of them as they are. It shows our trust that they are able to handle their own lives, without our trying to change them or teaching them how to live, act, or think. Such an approach therefore contributes to an environment in which people have the best possible opportunity to make positive decisions about their own worth, to choose to raise their own self-esteem.

During the course of more than a quarter of a century as a pastor, I dealt with people through every imaginable form of disease and crisis. It became evident to me that what they wanted most was someone who cared to be with them at these ultimate moments. Neither money nor words nor Bible verses

---

[6] Henri Nouwen, *Out of Solitude* (Notre Dame, IN: Ave Maria Press, 1974), pp. 34–35. Copyright © 1974 by Ave Maria Press, Notre Dame, IN 46556. All rights reserved. Used with permission of the publisher.

[7] Ibid, p. 36.

health or a lost relationship or a lost reputation. All that can really help at times of peril or grief is to have someone who cares who will be with us through the horrifying pain and fear and loneliness and loss. The faith revealed in that person's willingness to be there with us, not running away from the pain and not giving superficial answers to questions that cannot be answered, gives us assurance that we matter, that we are worth the effort. We are loved. There is hope. We can make it.

We want that deep, personal caring at a lot of other times too but in our most stressed-out moments of crisis, this is what matters more than anything else. What we want most is caring companionship. Whoever we happen to be, we all want to know that we matter to someone. The way we know we matter is for someone to be willing to take the time to be with us: to pay attention to us and to listen even if at that moment we have nothing to say. This is the ultimate foundation on which to build and restore and maintain a vigorous and healthy sense of self-esteem.

Even Jesus, in his hour of greatest personal stress, found his comfort in the confidence that he was not alone. "The hour is coming, indeed it has come, when you will be scattered, every man to his home, and will leave me alone; yet I am not alone, for the Father is with me" (John 16:32).

One person we need very much to be with is our *inner child.* This refers to the child we once were, the child we were in the past who continues to live within us as a continuing part of who we are in the present. Researchers have compiled a massive body of evidence indicating that most of us, usually without our being aware that we are doing so, often respond to situations in our adult lives with the same fears, needs, values, and persepectives that directed our lives when we were kids. Before we can get on with our growth as adults, we need to acknowledge, listen to, and care for this aspect of ourselves, our inner child.

Chances are that this inner child suffered much from not having someone to be with him or her during important moments. That hurting and lonely child still longs to be recognized and cared for; and without that gentle caring, our inner child tends to provoke a good bit of suffering and confusion and misdirection in our lives today. Notice the amazing similarity between the paragraph we read from Nouwen on what it means to be present to a friend in need, and the way Branden counsels us to care for our own inner child.

> We can learn to recognize that child, make friends with him or her, and listen attentively to what the child needs to tell us, even if it is painful. We can allow the child, in effect, to feel welcome within us, thereby allowing the child-self to be integrated into our adult-self.[8]

Having someone who cares to be with us is our ultimate human need. Not long after coming to this conviction, I made another significant and related discovery based on the scriptures of the Old and New Testaments. *God's ultimate promise to his people is that he will be with us.* He does not promise an easy life. The life of Jesus, whom Christians commit themselves to follow, was one of suffering and pain and loneliness and abandonment and, finally, a painful and humiliating death. It is not accurate to say that God promises palaces or gold or popularity or serenity. The foundational promise, given again and again, is: "I will be with you."

This promise appears in the Twenty-third Psalm, the one Old Testament passage that is best known to most

---

[8] Nathaniel Branden, *How To Raise Your Self-Esteem* (New York: Bantam, 1987), p. 16.

people, even to many who have no background or contact with a religious community. In some unique way, it has spoken for centuries to the deepest needs and longings of millions of people across a wide span of cultures and traditions. And this psalm's pivotal center is this thought: "Even though I walk through the valley of the shadow of death, I fear no evil; *for thou art with me*" (Ps. 23:4) (emphasis added).

Another instance occurred when Moses protested that he was not adequate to the task of leading the people of Israel out of their captivity in Egypt and into the Promised Land. This was God's answer: "But I will be with you" (Exodus 3:12). And in the first chapter of the first book of the New Testament, an angel spoke to Joseph about the son who would be born to Mary, and the name by which that son would be known. The angel did this by quoting and interpreting prophetic words from Isaiah: "Behold, a virgin shall conceive and bear a son, and his name shall be called Emmanuel (which means God *with us*)" (Matthew 1:23). As if to show the consistency of this promise from beginning to end, the very last line in the last chapter of that same Gospel tells of Jesus' final words, and final promise, to his disciples: "and lo, I am *with you* always, to the close of the age" (Matthew 28:20) (emphasis added).

In the very last book of the New Testament, the Revelation to John, in the final imagery of the new day that is to come, the believers are given this very specific description of the glory which they can expect:

> And I heard a great voice from the throne saying, "Behold, the dwelling of God is *with men.* He will dwell *with them,* and they shall be his people, and God himself will be *with them*" (Revelations 21:3) [emphasis added].

This promise had been the grounds for becoming disciples at the beginning of Jesus' ministry. In the first chapter of the Gospel according to Mark, Jesus had just begun his ministry. Passing by the Sea of Galilee, he saw four fishermen—Simon, Andrew, James, and John—and he called them to follow him. He told them nothing of how long they would be gone or where they were going or what might be in it for them if they were to follow. He asked nothing about their past or their capabilities or their interest or fears or what they believed. He gave Simon and Andrew only a very obscure description of the work he had in mind for them: "I will make you become fishers of men"; and he gave no description at all to James and John.

The only thing those four men knew when they got up and joined Jesus' journey to who-knew-where was that wherever Jesus was, they would be *with him*. That was enough. Apparently they trusted themselves enough to dare to be a part of that mysterious and unknown adventure, and they trusted Jesus enough to be willing to go wherever he might choose to lead them. The prospect of being *with him* was enough to make the journey before them worth the commitment of their lives. And the journey proved to be an experience of unparalleled wonder and growth and usefulness. They were witnesses to events that changed the way the world dated its years. For all the pain and disappointment and suffering that were a part of the journey, the stories they wrote indicate that those followers, among other things, came back feeling, "I wouldn't have missed it for anything!"

They were risk-takers, and taking risks is one of the most consistent items on any listing of the prerequisites and characteristics for healthy self-esteem. To be growing, maturing human beings, we need to nurture, encourage, and support risk-taking in ourselves and in others. People who are able to take risks have a sense of personal richness. They are participants in the adventure of being alive. They find their courage in having experienced themselves as being loved and having chosen to believe it is true. These people can take risks because, whatever may happen, they're not afraid that they'll lose everthing, or that their lives would be over if whatever it is they are risking doesn't work. Jesus' disciples, from Peter in the first century to Bonhoeffer in the twentieth, have been risk-takers. They are also people who have had authentic relationships of personal sharing with significant others. Because of their confidence in their *being,* they have been able to *do.* They are people who have chosen to believe they are loved.

What can I do to help? I can dare to be with other people in authentic relationships of caring. I can believe so ardently in myself and my own worth as a human being that I am free to be with others in their times of need, even though I have no answers or remedies. I can show people the depth and truth of my belief in them and their worth. This allows them the opportunity to believe in themselves and to take responsibility for their own lives, which is what it is to be an authentic human being. Effective doing flows forth from positive and authentic being.

This attitude of *being with* has important implications for our world view. Our task is not to impose our political or economic or religious convictions on the rest of the world. If we have a healthy and honest respect for ourselves, then we can respect the integrity of all other human beings also. We can act and vote in ways that protect and promote the dignity and worth of every human being. Alan Paton, an author and penal reformer from South Africa who was fighting for racial equality long before it had become a fashionable international issue, faced this question within his own life as a person and citizen. After explaining how he had come to his convictions about the possibilities for a nonracial unity through his personal relationships with people of different races, Paton asked:

> Now, is it possible or is it not possible to realize in society what one has realized in personal relation-

> ships? I believe one cannot answer the question. All that one can say is that there is within one an impulse to try to realize it, that this impulse is an intergral part of one's self, and that it must be obeyed, for to disobey it is to do damage to the integrity of one's self.[9]

"What can I do to help?" Take responsibility for your own self-esteem. Dare to be in touch with the painful and scary wounds that exist inside you. Learn to give yourself acceptance, understanding, and forgiveness. Learn to love yourself—to appreciate and enjoy the unique person you are. Then you will have put yourself in the best possible position to be a genuinely helpful person to others, being sensitive to their hurts and needs and acting in ways that give them the best possible opportunity to make positive decisions about themselves.

None of this happens all at once, nor is it ever complete. We are always in process, always becoming. A fuller experience of life and ourselves and the truth is always in front of us. to be alive, truly alive, is to be growing. "Love is the will to extend one's self . . .." The little girl going off to kindergarten extends herself to leave the familiarity and security of home to risk the adventures of life in a strange new world. Most of us made it to kindergarten, and probably to many other new worlds beyond that level of extending ourselves. Alas, many of us eventually came to a point when we quit moving on. We quit running risks. We decided to stay put, even if we didn't like where we were. Our lives became exercises in doing what is expected and required rather than adventures in being who we are and discovering who we are to become. When we quit being willing to run risks, we quit loving ourselves. And we quit growing.

---

[9] Alan Paton, "The Crisis of Fear" (*The Saturday Review*, Sept. 9, 1967), p. 46.

To turn it all around, to begin loving ourselves, means being willing to risk: to let go of old habits, old securities, old ways of looking at things, old ways of thinking. To love ourselves means to start growing again, becoming people who allow our doing to flow forth from our being, from a new choice: daring to believe that we are loved. Faith is never a habit. It is a decision that we make again and again.

CHAPTER NINE

What Does Healthy Self-Esteem Look Like?

Some writers and speakers have an amazing gift: the ability to use words to articulate needs or hopes or fears or longings we feel in the most personal depths of our beings but have not been able to grasp or explain, even to ourselves. Through the insights and definitions provided by these writers and speakers, we sometimes gain a deeper understanding of ourselves and a stronger foundation for the choices we need to make. Joseph Campbell, the world-renowned expert on myths, did this for me in three short sentences. Through his words a remote and misunderstood yearning that had long been a troublesome tenant near the core of my soul was transformed into a welcome and exciting friend.

> People say that what we're all seeking is a meaning for life. I don't think that's what we're really seeking. I think that what we're seeking is an experience of being alive.[1]

---

[1] Joseph Campbell, *The Power of Myth* (New York: Doubleday, 1988), p. 5.

The moment I read those words, something inside of me cried out "YES!" That same response happens with almost the same intensity even now, whenever Campbell's insight crosses my mind. After a lifetime of pondering, philosophizing, and searching, I recognize that my deepest longing is not for more philosophical explanations or psychological understandings but for an experience, an experience of being alive. I suspect that is true for most of us. Jesus understood that proofs and explanations were not our deep need. "I came that they may have life, and have it more abundantly" (John 10:10b).

With that in mind, this chapter seeks to go beyond explanations. As with Ezekiel's dry bones, I want the words about self-esteem and spirituality to come alive through their connections with real people whose loving regard for themselves is experienced in the healthy purposes of their lives and their nurturing contacts with others.

Bradshaw had it right: "They [children] need a face to mirror and affirm their feelings, needs, and drives."[2] A face. The affirming that children, and all of us, need so desperately is an experience that cannot happen through a lecture or a book or a set of rules. The deeply profound affirmations that change a person's life can happen only through a face, a person: through the love and respect and acceptance and understanding and I-am-here-with-you-and-for-you feeling that radiate and communicate through a nurturing human presence.

This psychological reality is, for me, one of the most exciting truths of the Christian faith, even though it is consistently missed, ignored, or forgotten. Being a Christian so

---

[2] John Bradshaw, *Healing the Shame that Binds You* (Deerfield Beach, FL: Heath Communications, 1988), p. 56.

easily becomes a matter of living by certain rules, defending certain doctrines, fighting over the precise interpretation of certain verses of scripture. Religious words have been used to justify slaughtering people by the thousands, burning heretics and witches at the stake, condemming and convicting and ostracting—all in the name of the eternal God. What gets lost in the push and pull of being Christians is that the whole movement began when some fishermen were compellingly attracted, not to a philosophy of life or a set of rules, but to a face—to a person who looked at them and into them and said, "Follow me."

In the biblical story, this is God's plan for saving the world: He came as a person to be with us. He did not send a book or deliver a lecture. In Jesus Christ, God has a face, a human face, in which we see mirrored and affirmed our eternal dignity and worth as persons. God's fullest and finest definition of what it means to be a human being cannot be contained in any set of words. It can only be expressed and experienced in a human life. In Jesus Christ we see what an authentic human life looks like. "This is my beloved son; listen to him" (Mark 9:7b).

That's always been a problem for us. Christians talk a lot about living by faith, but few of us have any real appetite for living by faith. Something within us wants certainty! We want the truth in words and propositions. With words we can prove—absolutely and with finality—who's right and who's wrong, who's in and who's out, who's saved and who's damned, who's pleasing to God and who's an infidel.

Yet the Gospel according to John says specifically what the entire New Testament affirms, namely, that God's Word to us is not a word but a living human being: Jesus Christ. "The Word became flesh and dwelt among us" (John 1:14a). That's very frustrating. Having a person as our measure of what God wants, rather than words, means we have far less certainty in proving who's right and who's wrong. It also means we're thrown back on ourselves to make a lot of decisions that we can't be sure of until after we've made them—if even then. It means we have to make personal choices, take responsibility for them, and then face up to the reality that sometimes we're wrong.

The measure of what God wants our lives to be is a human life, and not a precise set of rules. We therefore live in the world not by knowledge but by faith. We trust we are loved without being able to prove it. We have faith that life has meaning while acknowledging there are times when that meaning can't be seen or heard or touched anywhere. We live by trusting that loving is better than controlling, even when it appears that the power-brokers of the world have everything going their way. We trust it is better to be a human being with the responsibility to make choices than a machine that simply obeys orders. We value having those choices even when we're feeling much pain and disappointment and bewilderment and despair as a consequence of them. We trust that the joy we once experienced as human beings and the joy we hope to experience again make it worth enduring any necessary pain we may have right now. We have a living model for all this in the life and person of Jesus.

Having insisted, with words, that truth can never be fully contained within any words, I must acknowledge that words are indispensable in our quest for understanding. Christians use words to discuss the meaning of that human life God gave us as a measure of what it means to be human. We need not seek an escape from using words, but we must use them with the clear recognition that even the very best of words—the most accurate and the most expressive words possible—have their limits, and they can never fully express the truth.

We can select and use our words very carefully, grateful for the insight and direction they give and acknowledging their limits. It is important to remember, though, that the compass God has given in our search for truth is a person. Listening to Jesus—to anyone—involves far more than hearing words. Empathetic listening requires a commitment to search for an understanding of the meaning behind the words. It means listening with the intent to understand, emotionally as well as intellectually, rather than looking for loopholes or justifications. Active listening means being open to the possibility of being changed by what we hear: changed in our perspectives, attitudes, understandings, behaviors.

Sometimes we can become personally involved in the words in a book. Listening to a person has an even deeper dimension. To listen actively and respectfully to a person demands a willingness to be personally vulnerable to that person and his or her meanings. We might be changed. No wonder we so often settle for words. No wonder people have always attempted to reduce the Word to a set of words.

What's more, those who believe that Jesus Christ is the fullest expression of God's truth are tipped off that the truth is never a simple, black-and-white declaration. It is paradoxical. In John's gospel, for instance, Jesus says, "I am the Truth." Is Jesus, the Truth, fully human or is he fully divine? Throughout the centuries, the church has maintained he was both—at the same time. How can that be? The Truth is a paradox, and so is every other truth.

Should children be given unconditional love, or should they be given a known structure with limits and expectations? Both. In fact, to give either one without the other is to do the child a great disservice. The truth is paradoxical: not one or the other, both! What seems like a contradiction turns out to be a profound truth. As frustating as this often is, it's another reason why the truth can never be reduced to a sentence or a slogan or a single point of view. A strong human being, for example, cannot be described simply as vulnerable and caring, nor simply as inner-directed and self-reliant. The truly strong person is both, as contradictory as those sets of characteristics seem to be.

Self-esteem itself demonstrates the paradoxical nature of truth. For example, we have convincing evidence that the family in which we grow up is the source of our self-esteem. It is also true, however, that when we become adults, we are totally and personally responsible for our self-esteem, regardless of what our past experiences have been. We need to recognize the importance of the family influence for the sake of our own children and in order to understand how we got to where we are today. We also need to take seriously that we are personally responsible for our own self-esteem or we'll get stuck living with a victim mentality, blaming all or problems on someone else. In looking at life and at ourselves, we need to understand that all truth is paradoxical.

What follows is a list of the seven most prominent characteristics I see in people with healthy self-esteem. They are in couplets or triplets, to represent an awareness of the paradoxical nature of truth.

1. ACCEPTANCE AND AMBITION

Self-acceptance is the core characteristic of people with healthy self-esteem. This quality is at once the most necessary and the most difficult to acquire. Self-acceptance is necessary because no growth occurs without it and difficult because most of us have exerienced very little genuine acceptance in our lives—so little that we know acceptance more as a concept than an experience. Until we have experienced the miracle of acceptance from someone outside ourselves, self-acceptance does not even exist as an option for us. Yet, until we have chosen it as an attitude or process for dealing with ourselves, we can have no personal growth. Putting ourselves in a position to experience and receive acceptance is therefore an absolute necessity.

When I meet self-accepting people, I can feel it in them almost immediately. I sense it because, having accepted themselves, they are also accepting of me. I do not feel myself being measured or judged. They are personally and genuinely interested in me, and their interest is in knowing and appreciating, not in judging or assessing. This allows me to relax in their presence.

In the comfort of being accepted, rather than worrying about how I am doing, I find myself able to be more accepting also—of myself and of others. Because I am less anxious about "how am I doing?" I can pay more attention to the people around me and what they're thinking and saying and doing. Self-accepting people are at peace with themselves. They aren't trying to impress or prove or intimidate. Some of the words that come to mind are: genuine, relaxed, present, vital, reasonable, intuitive, sincere, spontaneous, caring, deep, present, honest, comfortable, aware, understanding, creative, flexible, independent, sensitive, confident, humble, joyful.

In living with or working with self-accepting people, I notice that they easily acknowledge their mistakes and go to work correcting them without condemning themselves or being pressured by excessive guilt. Because they're not clinging to any particular image of themselves, they are able to receive new insights with delight. With genuine appreciation, they make changes in their way of thinking and acting.

This is the sense in which self-accepting people are also ambitious. Their basic joy in being alive, even in the midst of difficulties and pain, makes them eager (ambitious) to live— ever more fully, lovingly, and capably. They yearn to be ever more deeply in touch and involved with the depths in themselves, in the people with whom they live, and in the mystery of life around them.

People with healthy self-esteem are not ambitious in the sense in which we usually hear the word used. Because they accept and appreciate themselves as they are, they don't waste their energies striving for goals for the sake of enhancing their status in society or fulfilling an anxious need to prove their personal worth. They don't even compete with themselves, as if they need to prove to themselves how capable they are or how much they can achieve. Their ambitions are to be ever more fully alive within themselves and ever more fully a part of the life going on around them. They rejoice to share with others their excitement about being alive, welcoming and encouraging the aliveness of others.

Self-acceptance does not mean we're satisfied with how we are and have no desire to change and grow. Self-acceptance means we acknowledge that where we are now is where we are now. It's the reality of our lives. It's how things are. Acceptance avoids judgmental words like "wonderful" and "horrible" and acknowledges what "is." Looking at things precisely as they are is what allows us to make reasonable and appropriate decisions about what we want to change.

This paradoxical relationship between self-acceptance and change is the foundation of Alcoholics Anonymous and all the Twelve-Step programs. Until a person can take the first step, by saying, "I am an alcoholic," thereby recognizing that a problem does exist, he or she cannot make any plans or take any appropriate actions to deal with that problem. Once the person has accepted him- or herself, acknowledging how things are, then that person can create and pursue reasonable expectations, that is, can become the genuine human being he or she is destined to be.

2. NURTURANCE AND RESPONSIBILITY

The gestalt psychologist Fritz Perls once observed that there are only two kinds of people in the world: the nurturing and the toxic. He advised that we spend as much time as possible with the nurturers and steer clear of the toxic. This division is far too simplistic, yet it makes a significant point. There *are* people in whose presence we experience ourselves being supported and fed. With others, we feel ourselves being buffeted and drained.

In his keynote address to the closing conference of the California Self-Esteem Task Force, Ken Blanchard reported this his wife, Marjorie, who works with him in his business consulting organization, had done a study and determined that "Bad bosses make people sick—literally sick." Intrigued, Blanchard himself launched a two-year endeavor to find out what constitues a "bad boss."

In his study, Blanchard found that two types of bad bosses predominate in the United States. The first type is ineffectual and uninvolved, unwilling to step forward to make decisions and take responsibility. The second type is even more numerous. These are the bosses who overcontrol. They're always right and prove it by showing that everyone else is wrong. "What's really interesting about both these types," said Blanchard, "is that both of them are classic examples of people with low self-esteem."

People with low self-esteem are toxic, not nurturing. They spend their energies seeking to prove that their painful, unacceptable, and often unacknowledged feelings about themselves are not warranted. They attempt to achieve these proofs at the expense of whoever happens to be around them: spouses, children, parents, siblings, pupils, coworkers, friends, employees, employers.

Jim Newman, author of *Release Your Brakes*, suggests becoming the kind of persons that others look forward to being with again. Perhaps that thought brings some people to your mind, people in whose presence you have experienced yourself as prized and appreciated, coming alive. We see this quality in Jesus. Even though he had absolutely no status or credentials, and no mass media by which to advertise his fame, he attracted people by the thousands. Something about him made people want to be with him: to see him, to hear him, to touch him. The crowds surrounded him in such numbers and so unrelentingly that it was frequently necessary for him to take extraordinary measures to get away from their demands so he could nurture himself.

Nurturing people do nurture themselves. They also put themselves in contact with people and situations that will nurture them. None of us have an inexhaustible supply of attention and caring and listening to give, and neither did Jesus. He carefully made sure he had time to stay in touch with God, with himself, and with a nurturing fellowship of friends. He then had the energy and resources to share with others. Love seems to be one essential that human beings cannot create. We can only receive it and share it.

Not all people wanted to be with Jesus. On the contrary, some felt painfully uncomfortable in his presence, so much so that they threw their energies into plotting to destroy him. His insistence on being responsible made these people so uneasy that they had to get rid of him. These were the people whose sense of worth depended on maintaining a front of superiority to others, as in political power or righteousness before God. Jesus' authenticity exposed their pretentiousness, their lack of integrity. The power of his honesty and his genuine concern threatened to destroy the defenses behind which they hid themselves and their fears.

Responsibility is thus the paradoxical partner of nurturance. Unconditional acceptance, essential as it is to self-esteem, is not enough. The growing child needs unconditional acceptance and a reasonable, dependable structure in which to develop. Truly nurturing people recognize this paradoxical need, in themselves and in others. So, along with giving understanding and compassion and encouragement, they live within a structure of responsibility.

A friend of mine was once in a relationship that was important to her but in which she felt herself being pushed out. In a fit of jealousy fueled by her low self-esteem, she climbed over an apartment fence to spy on the man who was mistreating her but for whom she longed. Later in life, she would beat herself emotionally over this incident. Eventually she learned to understand and accept the very legitimate needs for love and attention that had existed in her all her life but had never been met. Climbing over that fence was not the stupid behavior of a crazy person, as the little voice inside had been telling her. It was an irrational but perfectly understandable effort on the part of the starving child inside her to get the love she needed so desperately. To nurture that needy, wounded child, she learned to understand and accept herself: to hold that needy child with real caring and compassion.

As a part of nurturing herself, my friend also learned to take responsibility for herself and what she had done. She did climb over the fence. She did leave her daughter in less-than-adèquate care to do so. She did run the risk of being arrested for trespassing. She does have giant, unresolved needs for love and attention. And she has accepted responsibililty for finding reasonable, effective ways to meet those needs.

As discussed in an earlier chapter, we teach responsibility (which is a highly nurturing activity) by being responsible. This includes providing reasonable structures in which people of all ages are able to face and accept responsibility for their decisions and behavior.

3. VULNERABILITY AND STRENGTH

The Roman Catholic theologian and writer Henri Nouwen has a thoughtful and intriguing definition of spiritual growth:

> It is not the movement from weakness to power,
> strength, but the movement in which we become
> less and less fearful and defensive and more and
> more open to the other and his world, even when it
> leads to suffering and death.[3]

This may contradict our perceptions. Most of us assume that to grow includes becoming stronger. We assume that when we finally "grow up," we'll no longer be feeling weakness, fear, uncertainty, or doubt. What if we began to think of growth as being less defensive? What that requires, of course, is a different kind of strength. It is the strength of believing we can make it in the world even though we acknowledge our fears, doubts, and uncertainties, even though we make mistakes and fail, even though we don't have all the answers. It is the kind of strength that we fear will feel like weakness because we are allowing ourselves to be vulnerable.

To be vulnerable means choosing to share our most tender feelings and fantasies and fears and failures—first with ourselves, and then with other human beings. To be vulnerable is to be real, authentic, who we are, believing that who we are is enough. People with healthy self-esteem are, thus, the ones who are able to be vulnerable and who are capable of authentic relationships.

> Whenever we experience and acknowledge our
> deepest needs—for relationship, for touching and
> holding, for identification and belonging or for
> separateness, to nurture another, or for affirma-
> tion and valuing—and do so openly in relationship
> with another human, we are allowing ourselves to
> become vulnerable.... To need is to be vulnerable.

---

[3] Henri Nouwen, *Reaching Out* (Garden City, NY: Doubleday, 1975), p. 77.

> To care is to be vulnerable. This is the heart of humanness.[4]

All of us live with some kind and some degree of emotional protection. As young children coming into a dangerous and difficult world, we develop various ways to protect ourselves: by being pleasing, rebellious, compliant, secretive, achieving, whatever. Growing and individuating are processes of learning to acknowledge and remove various pieces of our armor. Only when we gain the courage to be in touch with our own most sensitive and tender selves, and then to open our selves to others, are we capable of loving relationships. As long as we wear the armor of protectiveness and defensiveness, we prevent ourselves from feeling fully, living fully, and loving. Loving is a highly risky and vulnerable activity. C. S. Lewis describes it with his amazing insight and brilliant literary skill.

> To love at all is to be vulnerable. Love anything, and your heart will certainly be wrung and possibly be broken. If you want to make sure of keeping it intact, you must give your heart to no one, not even to an animal. Wrap it carefully around with hobbies and little luxuries; avoid all entanglements; lock it up safe in the casket or coffin of your selfishness. But in that casket—safe, dark, motionless, airless— it will change. It will not be broken; it will become unbreakable, impenetrable, irredeemable. The alternative to tragedy, or at least to the risk of tragedy, is damnation. The only place outside Heaven where you can be perfectly safe from all the dangers and perturbations of love is Hell.[5]

---

[4] Gershen Kaufman, *The Dynamics of Power* (Rochester, VT: Schenkman Books, 1983), p. 114.

[5] C. S. Lewis, *The Four Loves* (New York: Harcourt, Brace, Jovanovich, 1960), p. 169.

People with high self-esteem are willing to run the risks of being vulnerable. Having decided that they are capable of living, and being aware that only through being vulnerable can they live fully, they choose to be open to their own feelings, to the feelings of others, and to the inevitable pains of life. Risking vulnerability also opens them to love and joy and meaning.

Parents with healthy self-esteem do not protect their children from all pain and hurt. They understand that pain and hurt are parts of life. Such parents are willing to sit with their children in the midst of those pains without giving easy comfort or stern admonishments. Children learn they can survive these "necessary pains" as discussed earlier. Such parents have the strength to believe that they can live in the midst of such pain, rather than avoiding it neurotically. Their children can thus experience and then develop that same confidence about themselves.

In his autobiography, the historian and philosopher Bertrand Russell listed the three great passions of his life: "the longing for love, the search of knowledge, and unbearable pity for the suffering of mankind." Looking back on his life from near its end, he acknowledged that when he saw others in the pains that "make a mockery of what human life should be," he longed to alleviate the evil—but he could not. And that was his suffering. Then he said, "This has been my life. I have found it worth living, and would gladly live it again if the chance were offered me."[6]

People with healthy self-esteem are willing to experience and express themselves openly because of their confidence that they are enough. In one of his most beautiful passages, the apostle Paul told the people of Corinth that his

---

[6] Bertrand Russell, *The Autobiography of Bertrand Russell* (London: Unwin Hyman, 1951), p. 4.

confidence in God gave him courage to be his authentic self, weak though he was. In that authentic weakness, he discovered his most genuine strength: "for when I am weak, then I am strong" (II Cor. 12:9).

How can weakness be strength? Look at the reverse. Imagine someone who seeks to give an impression of confidence by pretending to be all-knowing and strong. People intuitively sense the deception and recognize the fear from which it comes. Even if such a person succeeds in being intimidating, that facade deprives him or her of authentic relationships and personal sharing.

By contrast, those who are willing to be who they are—not so very strong, not always right, often bewildered and frightened—are the people who have a true inner strength. They are able to connect with other human beings at a deep place of meaning and truth.

4. FORGIVENESS AND HONESTY

People with healthy self-esteem are forgiving people, and they begin by forgiving themselves. When we hear the word *forgiveness*, almost immediately we may begin thinking how difficult it is. We know we're supposed to forgive those who have trespassed against us, but it's hard. The greatest difficulty in forgiveness usually is that we do not feel forgiven and have not forgiven ourselves. Even the Lord's Prayer connects our capacity to be forgiving with our experience of having been forgiven. We cannot give to others something we do not have in ourselves. Or, as a custodian once put it, "You can't no more say what you don't know than you can come back from where you ain't been."

Central to the Christian faith is the conviction that in Jesus Christ we are fully forgiven. Frequently in Jesus' parables and in his conversations with his disciples, he empha-

sizes the amazing totality of God's forgiveness and the necessity for his disciples to share the blessings of their experience
of forgiveness with others. Even from his cross, with his own
life running out, Jesus acted to forgive the people who were
crucifying him. The need to understand and to receive forgiveness, and to act in forgiving ways toward others, runs
through the entire dimension of human life, from violent evils
to everyday mistakes.

For example, healthy people accept and protect what
Dr. Gershen Kaufman calls their "inalienable right to make a
mistake." He says that as he has grown as a person,

> I now expect to make mistakes on a daily basis,
> mistakes of judgment. Expecting to make signifi-
> cant mistakes at least four times a day is more
> realistic than expecting to never make mistakes.[7]

Our mistakes are the basis for our learning. As discussed
in the previous chapter, Dr. Arthur Combs recommends that
we establish a new educational system that encourages mistakes. The freedom to explore and be creative, which always
carries the possibility of making mistakes, is the basis for new
learning and insights, as well as the means by which people
learn to believe that they're enough. If only we would create
this same freedom in each of our communities—from our
families through our schools, workplaces, and congregations.

One Christian bumper sticker I like announces: "Christians aren't perfect, just forgiven." What a vital understanding that is. As explained in great detail in an earlier chapter,
Jesus does not call his disciples to be perfect but to be whole,
genuine, authentic. The basis of the Christian faith is the
confidence that we are loved. In that confidence there is
freedom to explore, to grow. Christians are not stuck with
their failures or mistakes. They are forgiven.

---

[7] Op cit., pp. 33–34.

Years ago a pastor friend of mine acknowledged that he felt great distress over what he saw as his failures in relation to his son. My friend said he'd spent hours in great intensity of spirit beseeching God to forgive him for his failures. When I asked if he believed God's forgiveness, he said he did.

"Then why are you still stuck with this great remorse?"

"Because I cannot forgive myself."

People who cannot forgive themselves do not truly believe or accept the forgiveness of God. If we believe God's forgiveness, we would understand ourselves to be forgiven. We could forgive ourselves. This is another instance in which God needs to have a "human face" so that the experience of forgiveness may be real.

When people believe themselves to be forgiven, they do not have to hide from their mistakes and failures. In the acceptance of forgiveness, they can accept themselves. They can look honestly at what they have thought and done, which allows them to grow from those experiences instead of having to stuff them away out of sight.

Forgiveness is by no means a purely religious necessity. The noted psychologist Sheldon Kopp lists forty-three items of homespun wisdom, the last of which is: "Learn to forgive yourself, again and again and again and again...."[8] Only those who have learned to forgive themselves can be honest with themselves, think clearly, create new and more reasonable goals, benefit from their experiences, and forgive others.

Forgiveness does not mean acting as if nothing is amiss. Suppose, for example, you go to a friend whom you have wronged in some way and say, "I'm sorry. Please forgive me,"

---

[8] Sheldon Kopp, *If You Meet the Buddha on the Road, Kill Him* (Palo Alto, CA: Science & Behavior Books, 1972), p. 224.

and your friend says, "That's OK. It doesn't matter. Think nothing of it." Chances are you're not going to feel forgiven. Your friend has failed to take you seriously or to deal honestly with the painfulness of the separation. To confront and acknowledge the pain of a personal hurt is terribly difficult, for both the one who has been hurt as well as the one who inflicted the pain.

Christians are constantly reminded (though familiarity often dulls awareness) of the costliness of forgiveness. The cross is the continuing symbol of, on one hand, the unconditional and unlimited depths of God's love and, on the other, the extent to which that love had to go to restore the broken relationship. The forgiveness of God that Christians see actualized in Jesus Christ is not by any means a forgiveness that says, "That's OK. It doesn't matter." On the contrary, forgiveness is given at great cost. It does matter! It is a forgiveness that is completely honest about the pain and the severity of whatever has happened. That forgiveness says, "As painful as the offense may be, you matter to me more than what stands between us." Forgiveness recognizes life's deepest truth: You are what matters. Our relationship of love is what matters, more than pain or dignity or image or honor or reputation or anything else.

People with healthy self-esteem are people who have chosen to feel positive about themselves: about their worth, about their right to be treated with dignity and respect. They are not hounded by or hiding from their past mistakes and failures. They have honestly acknowledged and grown from those past mistakes and failures, and they willingly share the same honesty and forgiveness with others.

5. WHOLE-HEARTEDNESS, WHOLE-MINDEDNESS, WHOLE-BODIEDNESS

Early in my ministry we began hearing more and more about *holistic medicine.* This approach to health and healing emphasizes that human beings cannot be separated into parts—body, mind, emotions, spirit—but that we react to life and our own experiences as total organisms. An injury to the body affects the mind and emotions and spirit, and a distress in the mind has corresponding consequences in the body, emotions, and spirit. When we have a deep emotional distress, for instance, we frequently say such things as, "I can't sleep and I can't eat."

In light of the fact that our human totality is usually referred to as wholeness, it seemed strange to me that *holistic* began with an "h." Then I learned that the word holistic comes from the same root as *holy,* which in early English meant "strong, complete, total, healthy."

Isn't it amazing how associations change the meaning of a word? After centuries of stamping "Holy Bible" in gold on foreboding black leather and linking religion with separate-from-the-world activities and people, the word *holy* took on meanings that were the exact opposite of its original intention. When I was in college the disparaging title given to apparently weak and out-of-it students was "Holy Joe." And it was medical science that later invoked its original meaning.

People with healthy self-esteem are holistic rather than narrow in their thinking and their interests. They respect the worth and importance of their minds, their bodies, their emotions, their spirits. And they respect those capacities in other people as well.

Western civilization seems to swing back and forth about what it means to be human. At times we emphasize the mind and spirit, saying that the body and things material don't matter at all. At other times we commence a frenzied pursuit of physical pleasures, as in, "You only go around once in life. Get all the gusto you can." We seem to emphasize first the "little-lower-than-God" side of our human condition and then give ourselves completely to the grasshopper part of our nature. And, very often, the neglected portion of the human totality erupts with vigor and vast destructiveness. In recent years, for example, several nationally known TV evangelists have received much adverse publicity for their involvement in sex scandals and the amassing of giant personal fortunes. These are major contradictions to the spiritual values they professed and proclaimed with such singular and exclusive tenacity.

It is becoming more and more evident that people with healthy self-esteem—that is, those who feel positive about themselves as persons—are most likely to take care of their bodies through exercise and nutrition. These people also respect and nurture their mental, emotional, and spiritual capacities. They give themselves to be all that they are: whole-hearted, whole-minded, whole-bodied. They are also more likely to be in touch with the wholeness of others and to appreciate the sacred worth of the world of nature.

6. RISK-TAKING AND RELAXATION

People with healthy self-esteem take risks. They are not controlled by their fears. Life is always a risk, never a sure thing. People whose lives are controlled by fear cannot become fully involved in the dynamics of life because every participation in life carries with it the threat of death. To love someone, for instance, is to run the risk of being deserted or used or rejected, which is an experience of death. So fearful people, people with low self-esteem, either withdraw from life to avoid being hurt, or go into life surrounded by such a protective structure of defenses that they never really live. This defensiveness ends up being the same as withdrawing.

In a magnificent sermon called "Creative Insecurity," Paul Scherer identified risk-taking as essential to Christian living.

> It isn't safe to believe in the God of the Bible. Indeed it isn't safe to live! Security at its peak is

> little more than sterility. Only insecurity has some chance of being creative. It can never be overcome. It can only be resolved into some other brave risk for us to take. If your life is dull, you haven't been taking any. . . . Life doesn't want to be safe . . .. It wants to create something. It wants to breast some slope. It wants to be gallant. Insecurity is its heritage.[9]

What a different perspective for most Christians. We're more accustomed to hearing preachers tell us that our faith will give us absolute confidence and security. That promise is even used as a "come on" to win adherents to the faith. Yet, Jesus certainly never made any such promises to those whom he called to follow him into a life in which virtually everything was uncertain.

A similar point arose in the midst of my ministry during a lecture by a very wise professor of theology. He advised pastors to go wherever they were needed. Jesus went to people in their need, wherever they were and whatever their condition. He went to them and he touched them, and in his touch they found their healing. The professor told of the time that he received a call from the madam in a house of prostitution saying that one of her ladies was sick and dying. This terminally ill lady wanted a pastor to come talk to her and pray with her. The speaker shared with us the fears that went through him. What kind of disease did this woman have? What if someone saw him going in or coming out of that place? Then he thought, "What if I do not go? What message does that convey to the dying lady and to all the rest of the people in that house?" As a pastor and as a human being, he chose not to refuse.

Taking that risk was part of being alive in the world. There are, of course, some risks that are patently foolish and

---

[9] Paul Scherer, *The Word God Sent* (New York: Harper & Row, 1965), p. 209. Copyright © 1965 by Paul Scherer.

destructive—risks by which we sabotage our aspirations and ourselves. These risks are taken by desperate people, people who feel they have nothing to lose. Rather than taking risks as a means of entering more fully into life, these people take risks because they've given up on life. Their risk-taking is really a form of suicide.

The difference is one we can feel when we're in the presence of risk-takers. People who are taking wild, desperate, destructive risks are wild, desperate, and destructive people—people with low self-esteem. They are taking risks in a frantic effort to get something vital and alive into their lives, or to get out of life. I don't feel safe around people who are trying to prove something about themselves. It's usually something they don't really believe, such as how tough they are, or how smart, or how lovable, or how fearless. Their lack of regard for themselves communicates itself in a lack of regard for us as well.

By contrast, risk-takers with healthy self-esteem exude a comfortable feeling of being relaxed. They are not driven to take risks as if their lives depended on it. They take risks because they have chosen to do so, personally and thoughtfully. Believing in themselves and in the worth of being alive, they take risks to be personally involved with life and with other people. Believing they are loved, they risk being a part of loving relationships. They take risks not to prove themselves but to be who they are, to express who they are, and to experience being alive. As Scherer said, they realize life was never meant to be safe.

The risk-taking aspect of self-esteem is like the stacks of chips in front of players in a poker game. People who choose to believe in their competence and worth as persons are like the poker players who start with high stacks of chips. As a consequence, they are able to enjoy the game. When they are dealt an interesting hand, they're able to play it, to take some chances. They know that even if they lose the chips they risk on that hand, they won't be wiped out. Plenty of chips still remain in front of them. People with healthy self-esteem can risk involvement with life, not fearful of being destroyed even if they lose or get hurt in any particular experience. It's only in playing that there's any chance of winning.

On the other hand, people with low self-esteem are like poker players with only a small stack of chips. They'll be afraid to risk their meager reserves. To lose at all would be to lose everything. So they don't get involved, but they do feel angry at not being a part of the action. They resent sitting there feeling they're being denied the opportunity to participate while others are having fun. They make up excuses for themselves and angry judgments about others. Over a period of time, the people with low self-esteem tend to become bitter and cynical, feeling they don't get the breaks or opportunities that other people enjoy. Because they lack the confidence and courage to take risks, these people cannot relax. They never win, never experience the joy of being alive.

People with healthy self-esteem are relaxed about being loved, relaxed about their worth, relaxed about life being meaningful. From that secure foundation, they are able to take the kind of risks in growing and relating that prove to be most effective and essential in releasing more life into the world.

7. THANKFULNESS AND ASSERTIVENESS

No characteristic of a person with healthy self-esteem is more vital than an attitude of thankfulness. That thankfulness becomes the basis for other positive attitudes and activities in life. As one of the leading professors of pastoral theology in the country, Dr. Roy Fairchild, told our class of graduate students: "When you consider all the Christian virtues—faith, hope, love, forgiveness, and all the rest—you finally come to thankfulness; and thankfulness is the irreducible."

A person's level of thankfulness is almost incidental to how much that person has. Like self-esteem itself, thankfulness is a decision we make, a decision that reflects how we feel about ourselves in relation to life. If we measure our worth in terms of our possessions or attributes, then our sense of thankfulness goes up and down depending on our fortunes. In that case, what we call thankfulness would be merely a momentary relief from feelings of inadequacy and insecurity.

People who are truly thankful are people who treasure life as a mysterious and miraculous gift which they have neither earned nor deserved. Every experience of love becomes a moment of joy and grace. These people are not strangers to adversity or pain. Indeed, they have experienced all of what we call the darker side of life without evasion or excuse. Harry Emerson Fosdick, one of the most famous U.S. preachers of this century, expressed it this way:

> Here is a man who feels that no matter what he does he never can pay back the debt he owes. To be sure, there is injustice in his experience, and "so much for so much" too, but when life is taken as a whole, he feels that he has received what he never could deserve or earn. In all ages the finest living has come out of folks like that. . . . There is no such thing as a vital Christian experience without gratitude.[10]

People who prize themselves, their lives, the opportunity to grow and to learn and to love, are thankful people. As many of them exist in so-called lower economic conditions as in the higher spheres—perhaps more. I have talked to thoughtful visitors to some of the economically deprived countries in South America who speak of the amazing level of gratitude

---

[10] Harry Emerson Fosdick, *Riverside Sermons* (New York: Harper & Brothers, 1958), p. 174. Copyright © 1958 by Harry Emerson Fosdick.

they found there. Perhaps people who cannot measure their lives in terms of possessions are thereby able to be more sensitive to the wonder of being alive, of friendship, of sunlight, of food to eat and water to drink, of the changing wonder of the seasons, of birth, of opportunitites, of bodies that function in such miraculous ways, of sight and touch and hearing and smell and taste, of humor, of understanding in times of distress.

As we have seen in earlier chapters, a victim mentality is one of the surest signs of low self-esteem. It is also very close to a lack of gratitude. "What's the use of trying? Nothing makes any difference any way. The harder you work, the more disappointed you'll be. So crank back your expectations and gut it out as best you can. Life is a pitiful grind, and then you die." To use Fosdick's phrase, we'll find no great living in people like that.

Thankful people are the assertive people, the confident people. Thankful people find life worth living and want to be involved in it. Because they are thankful, they are not desperate to acquire more goods, titles, or popularity. But they are eager to give: to share their delight in being alive. Joyful confidence wafts about them, and they live with maximum skill and effectiveness.

Some Christians object to assertiveness and expressions of confidence as if these are unseemly contradictions to their image of humility. Their objections make it a question of either/or: Should a person be confident or humble? The answer is not one or the other but both. Neither has any validity when worn as a role. Martin Luther once said that "True humility never knows it is humble." True humility is an authentic trait of character in people who are aware of how much they've been given, aware that life itself is a miraculous gift. Their humility is not a cowed contrivance. It comes as a result of an honest awareness of reality. All that is most precious in our lives are gifts from God and other people.

In the same way, truly thankful people are also confident. They believe themselves to be loved. They have received and recognized those precious gifts. The miraculous gift of life has been given to them. They are able to live. They want to live. Their living can be a source of joy and hope to themselves and others.

Based on her own experiences and years of work with others as a psychiatrist, Jean Shinoda Bolen provides us with a beautiful expression of this quintessential human virtue:

> I move through my day-to-day life with a sense of appreciation and gratitude that comes from knowing how fortunate I truly am and how unearned all that I am thankful for really is. . . . Every time I see beauty around me I appreciate what I am seeing, and simultaneously I have this sense of appreciation—for being alive to have this particular moment.[11]

---

[11] Jean Shinoda Bolen, *For the Love of God* (San Rafael, CA: New World Library, 1990), p. 51.

CHAPTER TEN

The Good News

Many people who have heard the word *gospel* all their lives don't know that it means "good news." It does. Alan Richardson, one of the most universally respected Christian scholars of this century, writes:

> The English word *Gospel* (Anglo-Saxon, god-spell, "God-story") is used to translate the Greek *evangelion*, "good tidings" . . ..
>
> The gospel must always be received personally by faith. . .. For those who thus receive it the gospel is always "news," breaking in freshly upon them and convincing them afresh, though they may have heard and accepted it long ago.[1]

It's easy to see how the confusion or misunderstanding concerning *gospel* arises. A sizable portion of what people have heard and learned from their churches is anything but

---

[1] Reprinted with the permission of the Macmillan Publishing Company from *A Theological Word Book of the Bible* by Alan Richardson, editor. Copyright © 1950 by Macmillan Publishing Company, Inc. Page 100.

good news. "As everybody knows by now," writes novelist/
theologian Fred Buechner, "Gospel means Good News. Ironically, it is some of the Gospel's most ardent fans who try to
turn it into Bad News."[2] Too often the heritage passed on by
the church has been guilt and shame and judgment and threats
and condemnation and feelings of inadequacy and a multi-
plicity of fears.

So how can the gospel be phrased in a way that communicates its good news with accuracy and authenticity to the
people of our day? I believe that one sentence from Bernie
Siegel, as cited in the introduction to this book, offers an
exciting and relevant possibility. It gathers up the biblical
affirmation of God's unconditional love for all people and
translates that almost incomprehensible miracle into words
of profound simplicity:

"You are not that unloved child any more."

Once we understand it, how can we accept this life-
changing good news? How can it become a vital, functioning
part of our lives? Richardson's commentary offers the consistent testimony of the Christian tradition as to how people
are able to take it in: "The gospel must always be received
personally by faith." It's sound psychology. Only by choosing
to believe it can we allow the benefits of the good news to
become part of our lives. Self-esteem is a spiritual journey, a
conscious, deliberate choice to believe: "I am not that unloved child anymore. I am loved!"

Why is that so difficult? Surely there's nothing any of us
wants more than to be loved. Why can't we take that new
image in, quickly and easily? A big part of the answer is that
we have not experienced being loved—at least not to the

---

[2] Frederick Buechner, *Wishful Thinking* (New York: Harper & Row,
1973), p. 32. Copyright © 1973 by Frederick Buechner.

extent that we've felt inclined to translate it into our way of thinking and feeling about ourselves. More often, what love we have received has been arbitrary, inconsistent, and conditional. Our memories of not being loved are so unbearably painful that most of us are in a state of massive denial. Simply wanting to be different is not enough. Neither is it enough to keep saying positive words over and over again. Something deep down inside us, lodged in our personal experiences, doesn't believe it. The only way to reprogram our deepest beliefs about ourselves is to change the information being fed into our memory file, to give ourselves new experiences of validation and worth on which to make a more accurate and appropriate decision.

For most of us, our parents did the best they could, just as most of us are doing the best we can for our children. But the parenting we received and the parenting we give are rarely sufficient for fostering healthy self-esteem. Painful as it is for me as a parent to admit it, that's a reality. Yet, however inadequate the parenting we received, it is not an excuse for abdicating our personal responsibility and living a life of defeat and despair. To begin anew, to have more human, more fulfilling lives, we can begin by focusing and reflecting with our most vivid imaginations on the good news: we are no longer unloved children. We are loved.

Christians find the basis for that faith in the gospel of Jesus Christ. The affirmation of the Christian gospel is that the eternal God loves the people of this world so much that he came to be with them. He came to be one of them and one with them, to share their lives and their deaths. Even the pain of a humiliating death did not deter his love. To believe in Jesus Christ is to believe that we are loved and precious to the eternal God. His love is without limits or reservations; it is personal and eternally dependable. Love is our esssential need. Christians, however, have no monopoly on this theme. It is a common denominator among the world's great religions.

Psychiatrist Jean Shinoda Bolen says that changing our beliefs is what happens in psychotherapy. As a therapist and a student of Eastern wisdom, her prescription is: "We must transcend our own limiting beliefs in order to grow beyond them, or in order to have the experiences that will allow us to grow."[3] We need to experience being loved, and faith is the essential avenue for receiving that love.

Faith is not limited to people of religion. In his classic work, *The Art of Loving*, Erich Fromm goes to great pains to identify and explain himself as a "non-theist," which reflects his conviction that God is not necessary in his understanding of life. Yet, as his concluding argument, even Fromm insists that faith is our only hope.

> This process of emergence, of birth, of waking up, requires one quality as a necessary condition: *faith*. The practice of the art of loving requires the practice of faith.[4]

The "practice of faith" is an intriguing phrase, reminding us that faith is more than intellectual assent. Suppose we've worked out a personally satisfying answer as to where this good news comes from and have no more philosophical problems as to its truth. Why is it still so difficult to believe? I'm convinced this is the most serious problem of all—not the philosophical, intellectual, or theological questions, but the very mundane, practical problem of practicing our faith: learning (daring?) to see ourselves, and to act in the world, as people who are loved.

Many years ago, in a book long since out of print, I found one of the most helpful insights in this regard that has ever

---

[3] Jean Shinoda Bolen, *The Tao of Psychology* (San Francisco: Harper & Row, 1979), p. 76. Copyright © 1979 by author.
[4] Erich Fromm, *The Art of Loving* (New York: Harper & Brothers, 1956), p. 121. Copyright © 1956 by Erich Fromm.

come to my attention. I've carried this quote and its message with me through many years and into many different audiences and arenas, and it fits unerringly. Its author, psychiatrist Earl Loomis, raised the question of why it is so difficult for people to look into themselves. He answered by saying, first, that we fear "spooks and goblins" may be roaming around in our unexamined depths. "We refuse to plumb our depths because we fear that in looking for something good we shall find something horrible."[5] Nevertheless, this is not the primary reason we avoid searching into ourselves. "Mainly and paradoxically, the reason we refuse to search for our inner being is that we fear we shall find something good."

What? Afraid of finding something good? After several paragraphs of examining the incredible incongruity of this, Loomis explained:

> Basically, we resist recognition of our assets because, once recognized, they must be *used.* For goodness makes claims. It must be expressed. It must be used. Badness is goodness dammed up.[6]

What an insight! If we were to look into ourselves and discover that, in fact, we are lovable and capable people, we would lose the excuses behind which we hide. Once we acknowledge our strengths and assets, we must use them. We become responsible to be loving and capable persons.

Most of us have lived all our lives believing, to some extent or another, "I'm not enough." As painful and lonely and crippling as that low self-esteem proves to be, it has become a familiar and well-known way of life for us, a dependable if bothersome companion. We have structured our lives

---

[5] Earl Loomis, *The Self in Pilgrimage* (New York: Harper & Brothers, 1960), p. 5.
[6] Ibid, p. 6.

around a conviction about our scarcity. The way we communicate with others, the way we talk to ourselves, the way we relate, the way we work, the way we dream, the way we fight, the way we see the world, the way we believe or disbelieve in God, the way we interpret the past, the way we prepare for the future—all of it is built around that central belief: "I'm not enough." As disabling as that conviction may be, it is familiar. All too often, and ironically, we become accustomed to its discomfort.

Once we begin believing that "I am not that unloved child anymore," all that comfortable familiarity is lost. We can no longer go on feeling inadequate. We can no longer say, "I'd like to be more patient and more loving, but I don't have it in me." Once acknowledged, goodness has to be used. If we have capacities for love and patience, we must begin living as patient and loving persons, thus producing the new experiences in our memory banks that affirm: We *are* lovable and loving persons.

Practicing our faith, we will talk differently: no longer mumbling as if incompetent or being brashly assertive in an effort to cover our sense of incompetence. We can also talk to ourselves differently, no longer condemning and shaming ourselves for failures and no longer portraying ourselves as victims of circumstance. We can relate to other people differently: no longer afraid to be known, no longer feeling desperately inadequate and unworthy, no longer yearning to be someone else or despising those others who are (or seem to be) what we yearn to be.

Once we look into ourselves and find capacities for good, we can change our lives. We need no longer be stuck with unsatisfying jobs or inconsiderate friends or abusive relationships. We have choices. We can no longer blame others for holding us back. Being competent persons, having skills that are of benefit to the world, we know we can take risks to discover just who we are and where we belong. The voices out of our past say, "To seek to succeed is to risk failure." The new reality—the good news—is that, believing ourselves to be loved, we can afford to put ourselves into positions where failure and rejection are possibilities. We know that only in such positions are love and success real possibilities.

Yes, the real fear of looking into ourselves is the possibility of finding something good. Let's face it: Living with the conviction that "I'm not enough" gives us lots of excuses for blaming our parents and teachers and brothers and sisters and preachers and politicians for fouling up our lives, for feeling sorry for ourselves for being born so ugly or so short or so tall or so dumb. If I'm not enough, then I don't have to run the risks of loving or caring or learning or contributing or achieving. In many ways it's a much more comfortable life. To break out of all our old familiar patterns, to reexamine all our ways of thinking and talking and relating, to give up old excuses can be terribly painful and difficult. A new life is a possibility for us, but we cannot receive it without acknowledging and rejecting the old life we've been clinging to all our lives. We need to let go of the life that's supported and defined by the old messages of not being loved and not being competent, the life that carries with it myriad physical and psychological diseases.

Moving on to this new life is something like being an acrobat who comes to the moment when he must let go of his trapeze, turn completely around in mid air, and grab hold of the new trapeze that, he trusts, will be there waiting for him. To let go of his old trapeze is to release his hold on everything that has been his security, his source of support. After he lets go, while he is turning toward the new trapeze, he is without support, a scary time indeed. He makes his move in the *faith* that when he completes his turn the new trapeze will be there.

Do you see the parallels to our moving to a new and fuller life? We can't grab hold of the new life until we've released our grasp on the old one. If we don't let go, we'll continue swinging back and forth over the same old territory we've crossed so many times before, a life that's no longer appropriate or fulfilling. It's much easier not to let go, to find reasons not to practice faith, to continue telling ourselves, "There is no God. There is no love. I always have been a loser and I always will be, just like ——— always said. And there's probably no trapeze out there anyway." To let go of our familiar but destructive rhythms and routines so we can take hold of the confidence that "I am not that unloved child anymore" is difficult and frightening. It falls directly under Scott Peck's category of necessary suffering, cited earlier. But unless we endure that necessary suffering, we're stuck with the "old messages and their consequent diseases."

Suppose we decide we're willing to run those risks, what then? The first necessary act of faith is to picture ourselves in a new way, transcending our limiting beliefs: "I am not un-loved anymore. I am a loved human being." We need to picture and to think of ourselves as ones who deserve to be treated with dignity and respect. Then we need to act, to begin practicing our faith, that is, treating ourselves with dignity and respect. Both the envisioning and the enacting are acts of faith. Faith is the fundamental answer to raising our self-esteem, to becoming more whole and human persons. The first act is daring to believe "I am not that unloved child anymore"—to believe that we are loved. Collecting little pieces of love from our experience. Holding them together with the mortar of stories we have heard and books we have read. Focusing on that picture. Seeing ourselves within it.

The second act of faith is necessary for translating that picture of the new self into the actuality of being a new person. How do we find the faith to believe that we are loved? We experience and express that faith by doing. What's needed is faith enough to *act* on the basis of our new picture of our-selves, to live in the world as people who are loved.

The fourteenth chapter of the Gospel according to Matthew includes a marvelously insightful story that includes both these essential steps for attaining a healthier self-esteem. Jesus' disciples were out on the lake in a boat late at night, having been pushed far from the shore by a storm. They were frightened to see a mysterious figure walking toward them on the water. When Jesus assured them that it was he and not a ghost, Peter asked Jesus to bid Peter come to him on the water.

That's a crucial piece of the story. In asking Jesus to call him out onto the water, Peter was willing to entertain a new picture of himself, to think of himself as one who could actually walk on the water. Peter was willing to believe the impossible, willing to allow someone he trusted to help him create a new picture of himself doing something he'd known all his life he could not do. He was willing to believe he could be special and capable. "I am not what I thought I was." Jesus called him to come.

Now Peter was really on the spot. He could have stayed in the boat believing his little heart out, thinking of all the wonderful things Jesus could do, saving up exciting adventure stories to tell his grandchildren. He had the first faith down pat. He was willing to picture the possibility of being someone different, walking on the water. But what about the second faith? What about acting on what he believed?

Peter dared to move on to the second faith. He put one leg and then the other over the side of the boat. He got out. He was on the water. He dared to act on the basis of his new picture. Jesus told him he was able to do it, and Peter dared to believe it was so. He acted on his faith. He began walking on the water. Amazingly, it worked.

Then things got bad again. Walking on the water was not all fun and games. The waves began billowing up around him.

As Peter looked around, he saw himself surrounded by danger on every side. The water was slapping him in the face and stinging his eyes. The voices inside his head began to go to work on him. "What on earth are you doing out here? What an idiotic idea, thinking you could walk on the water. Your life may not have been all that great back there in the boat, but at least you were alive. Boring, perhaps, but at least you were safe and sound. You've always been a wild and impetuous oaf, but now you've really done it. This is curtains." As his faith began to slip, so did Peter—into the water.

Significant changes are always awkward, painful, and scary. Whether we're changing the way we grip our tennis racquets or the way we express our feelings, we move on to a new level of living only if we stick with it through that time of awkwardness and pain. If we give up and say, "It's just too difficult; I can't do it," we stay stuck where we are, hanging on to the old trapeze, going back and forth over the same old territory.

Just as he was about to go under, Peter looked back to Jesus. By putting himself back in contact with his source of confidence and hope, Peter again became able to function in this new way. He was back walking on the water. His new journey continued. Jesus asked him, "Why did you doubt?"

Jesus knew, of course, why Peter doubted. It's scary out there on the water, with huge and angry waves billowing up all around you, doing what you've never done before, what you've always believed it is impossible to do. It was a new journey, a new kind of life with new experiences and requiring new skills. Jesus knew because he had lived his own life in the midst of the impossible all the time: choosing the most unlikely people to be his followers and share his journey, making no effort to curry favor with the people in power, consistently standing up for the powerless and oppressed, and risking everything— literally everything—on the premise that love is stronger than hate, stronger than everything else, stronger even than death. Jesus understood why Peter doubted, but Peter needed to acknowledge and accept those doubts himself.

It is not strange that we doubt. There are obvious and defensible reasons for doubting the good news that we are loved. But for all the good reasons, the real issue remains: do I choose to allow my life to be controlled by my doubts or my faith? To move on or stay stuck? Those are the questions Peter had to face, and so do we. Are we willing to experience the death of old patterns and habits, the terror of the unfamiliar, to set out on the journey toward wholeness, fulfillment, and growth, to be the persons we are intended to be? It takes the practice of faith.

Though we seldom recognize it, we already live by faith, all of us. For most of us, our faith is that "I am not enough." It doesn't seem like faith. We've lived with it for so long that we think of it as reality, but it is merely a reality we have created— a reality that then gets supported as we live in ways that confirm it. If we believe I am not able to love, for example, I will not be able to love. My faith is therefore confirmed in my experiences. The basis for our thinking and acting is a matter of what we believe to be true about life. Acting according to our particular beliefs, we all live by faith.

Moving to a new life means believing something new about ourselves. For a while, our experiences in this new life seem awkward, strange, threatening, and painful, exactly as with Peter out on the water. So our new faith is tested severely after we make our decision. Sticking with it requires great persistence. It would be much easier to give up and say, "Well, it was a beautiful dream. The words sound good, but it simply doesn't work in reality." Change is awkward and painful, especially when we're changing something so fundamental as what we believe about ourselves and how we act. Fortunately, as Nathaniel Branden says:

> We can both enjoy our experience and find it strange—as if we are living in our body with a person we are not sure we know. To be able to accept some disorientation as an inevitable aspect of growth, and to be willing to tolerate it until we arrive at a new sense of the "normal," is essential to successful change.[7]

Chances are that many of the people around us are not going to be helpful as we make this change. Those people are scared too. They like their lives to be as predictable as possible, which includes being able to predict their friends (us). So if we begin being more confident than before, willing to take more risks, more open, more trusting, more hopeful, more excited about being alive, our friends aren't going to know how to deal with us. They may be annoyed when their old ways of treating us and talking to us no longer support their presuppositions about life and themselves. Our friends can make our efforts to change more difficult because our changes necessitate changes in them also. If we become new and different persons, we cannot expect our relationships to be the same as they were before. We may even lose some of our friends. While going through that experience, a friend of mine got in touch with his ambivalent feelings and recognized the impossibility of his dream. "I want a brand new life, and I want it without changing anything."

We may lose some friends, but we are also likely to make some new ones. There can hardly be a more appealing personal quality than an authentic confidence in one's ability to live. We find ourselves drawn to those whose sense of confidence comes from deep within, allowing them to keep their heads under pressure. These people seem fair in their judgments and dependable in their caring. We feel ourselves restored and nurtured in being with them.

---

[7] Nathaniel Branden, *How to Raise Your Self-Esteem* (New York: Bantam, 1987), p. 157.

As noted in an earlier chapter, a community of supportive relationships is of invaluable assistance during the time of venturing forth into a new world. To be surrounded by companions who share our new journey, who are committed to growth, helps keep us in touch with our own sources of confidence and hope. Their practice of faith supports our own. When Peter got scared and lost his faith, he began to sink. When he looked back to Jesus, his faith was restored and he again found his ability to walk on the water. A nurturing community is necessary to our growth.

Change can be frightening, even when it is a change for which we yearn. Most people stay stuck with an old, unsatisfying life rather than expose themselves to the pains and uncertainties of a new and healthy life. One of the defenses behind which we hide to avoid the rigors of change is to argue, "This all sounds so theoretical, so academic. How does it work when it is exposed to the reality of the world as it is? What evidence do you have that these truths are practicable in the real world?"

I find it of more than passing interest that one of the most active sources of support for the self-esteem movement is the world of business. People in business are certainly concerned with "reality." They look to the bottom line: the measurable results of their choices. What works is what matters, not pretty philosophical ideas. Ken Blanchard, who works with the top management of U. S. businesses, says the single most important change corporate America needs to make is to develop structures and systems that "help people to feel good about themselves—to help people win."[8] I think that means believing and acting on the good news, creating opportunities for people to make more appropriate and more positive deci-

---

[8] Self-Esteem Summit Conference, California Task Force to Promote Self-Esteem, and Personal and Social Responsibility, held in Sacramento, CA in June 1990.

sions about themselves, in an arena that is about as "real world" as you can imagine.

Blanchard examined what happens when we measure the business world by the standard of self-esteem. Companies differ in implementing the idea that every individual human being deserves to be treated with dignity and respect. The traditional American business pyramid, with the boss at the top and the workers at the bottom, is still useful in setting goals and objectives. Management needs to be receptive to input coming in from the ranks, says Blanchard, but it is still management's responsibility to determine direction. And then the pyramid needs to be inverted, which moves the workers to the top of the organizational chart, in a position to make decisions and to take responsible actions. The role of managers in this new arrangement is to be coaches and cheer-leaders, to help people win.

That's a scary idea for many managers. Are they willing to let go of direct control, to turn over many responsibilities to their employees, to accept a new function for themselves? Some are and some aren't. It all depends on their own levels of self-esteem. Blanchard gave two illustrations.

A friend of his went into an ice cream store in Atlanta. It was the middle of the morning, and he was the only customer. The clerk said, "May I help you?" and the man replied, "Give me a minute to decide what flavor I want." While he was considering his options, an older worker walked up to the clerk, whispered in her ear, and walked away again. The clerk then said, "You're going to have to take a number." The man responded, "What do you mean take a number? That's crazy! I'm the only customer in the whole store."

The clerk replied, "It's company policy." When the man continued to protest, she leaned over the counter and whisp-ered, "Please don't get me in trouble. She's my boss." The man decided to play along, and he took a number. It was 30.

The number showing on the sign was 27. The clerk called out, "28, 29." When the clerk reached his number, the man turned in his ticket and said, "I've decided I'm not hungry any more."

On the way out of the store, he stopped by the older woman and said, "Why did you put that young girl in such a humiliating position?"

With anger, the woman replied, "If you can't get them to obey the rules in the easy times, how can you expect them to obey when the crowds are heavy and the pressure is on?"

Here's an obvious case of a worker being humiliated, degraded, and demeaned, and having her intelligence and feelings ignored as the impersonal dictates of management are imposed from the top of the old pyramid. This is what happens when we choose to stay stuck with an old system, where policy (control) is given priority over the dignity and worth of persons. No one risks. Nothing changes. People continue to be sliced up and destroyed by the gears of an old, controlling structure. Such conditions make it difficult for a person to believe that "I am not that unloved child anymore."

In contrast to that story, Blanchard told of an experience he had with Scandinavian Airlines System (SAS). While he and his family were in Stockholm, they changed their travel plans and so needed to change their tickets from SAS to Swiss Air. At the airport as they were leaving, the baggage for all airlines had to be checked through SAS. The SAS worker to whom they gave their baggage said, "May I see your tickets?" The Blanchards explained they didn't have their amended tickets yet. The clerk replied, "I'm sorry but I can't check your baggage until you have the proper tickets."

Blanchard gave one of those big, long, disgusted sighs and said, "OK, tell me where I have to go to get my tickets changed."

The clerk looked at them for a moment, then smiled and said, "Why don't you folks just sit down here, and I'll see if I can get your tickets changed for you." She took their tickets and walked across to the other side of the huge terminal. They watched her go past the long line of people queued up at the Swiss Air counter. In a few minutes she reemerged, came back across the terminal, handed the Blanchards their tickets, and said cheerfully, "Now I can check your baggage for you."

Blanchard got her name and wrote a card about what she had done. The man who had recently taken over as the president of the company was a personal friend of Blanchard's who had moved SAS from the brink of bankruptcy to being one of the most prosperous airlines in Europe. He focused his attention on "moments of truth," those times when employees interact with customers in ways that convey impressions about the company and its character. The success of SAS was evidence that those are the moments that make or break the company.

Blanchard heard later that the company president had gotten a band, marched them to that clerk's station, and handed her flowers and tickets for a weekend vacation. He followed Blanchard's advice to "catch people in the act of doing something right" and his own maxim to support "moments of truth." Experiences like this give people reason for reflection, for reassessing old judgments about themselves, and for choosing to believe that they are loved, worthwhile, capable human beings deserving of respect and consideration.

This employee worked in an organization that gave her the freedom to make decisions and empowered her to take responsibility for meeting customers' needs. Management had faith in her and expressed it. She chose to have faith in herself—and to act on that faith. The organization was willing to run the risks of change, and the young woman dared to change also. It was risky. She was taking a chance. There was no organizational manual to cover what she did. She acted differently because she dared to think of herself as a capable person, able to make responsible decisions. The management style of her company encouraged such thoughtful, personal service. That policy not only heightened employee morale, it also brought the company from near bankruptcy to a dominant position in the industry.

This is what happens when we commit ourselves to helping people win. Whether in companies, schools, churches, or homes, we can help create environments in which people are allowed to experience the good news: that they have personal worth and effectiveness. Creating environments that offer people the best possible opportunity to make positive new decisions about themselves always involves risk. The managers at SAS had to face the possibility of organizational anarchy if employees began leaving their work stations to act on personal whims. The clerk risked criticism by choosing to act in a new and unprecedented way. It requires faith to change and grow, but change is possible. It does happen.

Learning to take risks is difficult and frightening for most of us. I've received personal benefit from this poem by an unknown author:

> To laugh is to risk appearing a fool.
> To weep is to risk appearing sentimental.
> To reach out for another is to risk involvement.
> To expose feelings is to risk rejection.
> To place your ideas, your dreams before the crowd
>   is to risk ridicule.
> To love is to risk not being loved in return.
> To live is to risk dying.
> To hope is to risk despair.
> To try at all is to risk failure.

But risks must be taken because the greatest hazard
   in life is to risk nothing
The person who risks nothing does nothing, has
   nothing, is nothing.

He may avoid suffering and sorrow, but he simply
   cannot learn, change, feel, grow, love, live.

Chained by his attitude, he is a slave. He has
   forfeited freedom. Only a person who risks is
   free.

A new life is available to us as persons, as families, as
communities, as a country, as countries in this one world. It is
a new life open to those who dare to picture and believe that
they are loved, who are willing to live out that faith in the way
they act and deal with others. This is where the Golden Rule
kicks in with such magnificent vitality: people who believe
they are loved go around treating others in a way that lets
them know they are loved. They show attitudes of dignity and
respect toward every person they meet: the members of their
families, their colleagues and neighbors, the clerks in stores
and restaurants, and people of all races and religions and
political persuasions. These are the nurturing people, the
ones who fill the atmosphere around them with hope and
creative energy. Because they believe they are loved, these
people are authentically loving.

Concern for others that comes forth from a constrained
sense of responsibility or as a painted-on effort to appear
beneficent doesn't nurture freedom or hope. Those who receive it experience it as manipulative and confining. When
people feel they are giving the last ounce of love they have
within them, their love is as tight and confining as the strained
looks on their faces. But people who dare to live out their
conviction that they are loved create a new world of freedom
and hope for those around them. The love and concern they
give are a genuine expression of who they are. How life-giving

it is to be loved by people who are giving from their overflow, not from their scarcity. These people give of themselves from their own joy in being alive. What they have to give is gratitude, hope, meaning, and a sense of excitement.

People whose lives are grounded in the faith that they are loved do more than change the atmosphere around them. In the ways they vote and in the causes they support, they are also creative participants in building a new world. My favorite understanding of *justice* is that it is love operating at long distance. People who believe they are loved are the ones who feel genuine concern for the homeless and hungry, people they may never know or even see in person. Their advocacy of social causes is not a compulsively driven effort to compensate for feelings of depravity or guilt, but a truly personal and compassionate concern for the dignity and worth of all human beings. Because they are drawing on a resource of love from deep within them, these workers for social causes are not nearly so likely to burn out in the frustration and exhaustion characteristic of those who are fueled by their anger, who are driven by their need to be noticed or to get even.

As our world becomes increasingly complex and threatening, there is a growing tendency to give up in hopeless despair. What can I do? What hope is there? How can any one person hope to make any difference in the face of such overwhelming odds? A more creative question is: How can I be a positive influence in such a world? People who dare to believe they are loved and who dare to be loving make a positive difference for good, even in a stressful and scary world such as ours.

But who are those people? Here's an important clue. Scott Peck has a sentence which he says came from his unconscious in the midst of a personal crisis when he was fifteen years old. It is one of the most ponderable sentences I've ever read in my life:

The only real security in life lies in relishing
life's insecurity.[9]

At first those words may seem to imply there is no
security, but that's not what they say. They state clearly that
there is a real security. It requires being willing, and more
than willing—excited—to live in full recognition that we do
not have all the answers and never will. We don't know what's
going to happen to us or to the world. Yet, when we believe we
are loved, something within us wants to live, to be a part of
that uncertainty, and even relishes it.

What kind of people can enjoy such monstrous uncertainty? Only those whose faith decision is: "Who I am is
enough. I am a loved and lovable and capable person. I am
competent to live. I want to live."

But why does Peck call that great uncertainty "security"?
From my faith perspective, I think it's because living in that
uncertainty, loving and choosing and feeling, we discover that
that's where we are meant to be. It's security because in that
situation we are fulfilling our destiny, being the persons God
created us to be, living the life we were created to live. Living
in uncertainty is right for us, being creatures in a world we did
not create but which was (and is) created by God, who loves
and cares for us personally and wants us to be here. It's the
security of being who we are. It's a life available only to those
who esteem themselves enough to choose it, to make the
journey.

To be alive is to be growing, risking, changing. Seldom
do significant changes in our lives happen all at once. More
often it is a matter of making the decision to picture ourselves
in a new and more positive way; then, on the basis of that new
decision, choosing to move in a new direction, to relate to

___

[9] M. Scott Peck, *The Road Less Traveled* (New York: Simon &
Schuster, 1978), p. 136. Copyright © 1978 by M. Scott Peck, M.D.,
P.C. Reprinted by permission of Simon & Schuster.

people, opportunities, challenges in a new way. Then the day comes when we look back and discover that we are different, that our lives are different. Achieving healthy self-esteem is a life-long journey. It is a spiritual journey in which we continually make new choices of faith and then dare to act on those choices.

The late Joseph Campbell, one of the world's most respected authorities on the history of myths from all countries and all cultures, spoke a deep truth when he said:

> If you do follow your bliss you put yourself on a kind of track that has been there all the while, waiting for you, and the life that you ought to be living is the one you are living. When you can see that, you begin to meet people who are in the field of your bliss, and they open the doors to you. I say, follow your bliss and don't be afraid, and doors will open where you didn't know they were going to be.[10]

Don't be afraid, in other words, or at least don't be controlled by your fears. Choose to believe in yourself. Dare to make the journey. Practice your faith. You have what it takes. You are a lovable, capable person. You can walk on the water. You can live. Go for the bliss!

> And I said to the man who stood at the gate of years,
> "Give me light that I may tred softly into the unknown."
> And he replied, "Go out into the darkness and put your hand into the hand of God.
> That shall be to you better than light, and safer than a known way."
> Anonymous

---

[10] Joseph Campbell, *The Power of Myth* (New York: Doubleday, 1988), p. 120.

BIBLIOGRAPHY

Barclay, William. *The Gospel of Matthew, Vol. 1.* Philadelphia: Westminster Press, 1975.

Becker, Ernest. *The Denial of Death.* New York: The Free Press, 1973.

Betti, Ugo. *Three Plays.* New York: Grove Press, 1958.

Bolen, Jean Shinoda. *The Tao of Psychology.* San Francisco: Harper & Row, 1979.

———.*For the Love of God.* San Rafael, CA: New World Library, 1990.

Bonhoeffer, Dietrich. *The Cost of Discipleship.* New York: Macmillan, 1949.

Branden, Nathaniel. *Honoring the Self.* New York: Bantam, 1988.

———.*How To Raise Your Self-Esteem.* New York: Bantam, 1987).

Bradshaw, John. *Healing the Shame That Binds You.* Deerfield Beach, FL: Heath Communications, 1988.

Buechner, Frederick. *Wishful Thinking.* New York: Harper & Row, 1973.

California Task Force to Promote Self-Esteem, and Personal and Social Responsibility. *Toward a State of Esteem.* Sacramento, CA: California State Department of Education, 1990.

Campbell, Joseph. *The Power of Myth.* New York: Doubleday, 1988.

Clarke, Jean Illsley. *Growing Up Again.* San Francisco: Harper & Row, 1989.

Coburn, John. *A Life to Live, A Way to Pray.* New York: Seabury Press, 1973.

Covey, Stephen R. *The Seven Habits of Highly Effective People.* New York: Simon & Schuster, 1989.

Dyer, Wayne. *Your Erroneous Zones.* New York: Avon, 1977.

Elkins, Dov. Peretz (Ed.). *Glad To Be Me.* Rochester, NY: Growth Associates, 1989.

Far West Laboratories. "Long-Range Impact of an Early Intervention with Low-Income Children and Their Families." San Francisco, 1987.

Fosdick, Harry Emerson. *Riverside Sermons.* New York: Harper & Brothers, 1958.

Fox, Matthew. *Original Blessing.* Santa Fe: Bear & Company, 1983.

Frankl, Viktor. *Man's Search for Meaning.* Boston: Beacon, 1959.

Fromm, Erich. *The Art of Loving.* New York: Harper & Brothers, 1956.

Ginott, Haim. *Between Parent and Child.* New York: Macmillan, 1968.

Glasser, William. *Reality Therapy.* New York: Harper & Row, 1965.

——.*The Quality School.* New York: Harper & Row, 1990.

Gordon, Thomas. *Parent Effectiveness Training.* New York: P. W. Wyden, 1970.

Greene, Brad. *Self-Esteem: A Manual for Helping Others.* Simi Valley, CA: 4 A-s Associates, 1989.

Haley, Alex. *Roots.* New York: Doubleday, 1976.

Institute for Noetic Sciences. *Noetic Sciences Review.* (Midwinter 1990). Sausalito, CA.

Kaufman, Gershen. *The Dynamics of Power.* Rochester, VT: Schenkman Books, 1983.

———. and Lev Raphael. *Sticking Up For Yourself.* Minneapolis: Free Spirit, 1990.

Keen, Sam. *Fire in the Belly.* New York: Bantam Books, 1991.

Kierkegaard, Soren. *A Kierkegaard Anthology.* Princeton University Press, 1946.

Kopp, Sheldon. *If You Meet the Buddha on the Road, Kill Him.* Palo Alto, CA: Science and Behavior Books, 1972.

Lewis, C. S. *The Four Loves.* New York: Harcourt, Brace, Jovanovich, 1960.

Loomis, Earl. *The Self in Pilgrimage.* New York: Harper & Brothers, 1960.

May, Gerald G. *Addiction and Grace.* San Francisco: Harper & Row, 1988.

May, Rollo. *Man's Search for Himself.* New York: Norton, 1953.

Naisbitt, John, and Patricia Aburdene. *Megatrends 2000.* New York: Morrow, 1990.

Nelsen, Jane, and Lynn Lott. *I'm On Your Side.* Rocklin, CA: Prima, 1990.

New World Library. *For the Love of God.* San Rafael, CA, 1990.

Nouwen, Henri. *Out of Solitude.* Notre Dame, IN: Ave Maria Press, 1974.

———.*Reaching Out.* Garden City, NY: Doubleday, 1975.

O'Conner, Elizabeth. "Faces of Faith," in *The Other Side.* 1990.

Paton, Alan. "The Crisis of Fear," in *The Saturday Review,* Sept. 9, 1967.

Peck, M. Scott. *A Different Drum.* New York: Simon & Schuster, 1987.

———.*The Road Less Traveled,* New York: Simon & Schuster, 1978.

Reid, Clyde. *Celebrate the Temporary.* New York: Harper & Row, 1972.

Richardson, Alan,*A Theological Word Book of the Bible.* New York: Macmillan, 1950.

Rogers, Carl. *On Becoming a Person.* Boston: Houghton Mifflin, 1961.

Russell, Bertrand. *The Autobiography of Bertrand Russell.* Boston: Atlantic-Little, Brown, 1951.

Satir, Virginia. *The New Peoplemaking.* Palo Alto: Science & Behavior Books, 1988.

———.*Self-Esteem.* Berkeley, CA: Celestial Arts, 1970.

Scherer, Paul. *The Word God Sent.* New York: Harper & Row, 1965.

Shostrom, Everett. *From Manipulator to Master.* New York: Bantam, 1983.

Siegel, Bernie. *Love, Medicine and Miracles.* New York: Harper & Row, 1986.

———.*Peace, Love and Healing.* New York: Harper & Row, 1989.

Tillich, Paul. *The Shaking of the Foundations.* New York: Scribner's, 1948.

Westberg, Granger. *Good Grief.* Philadelphia: Fortress, 1962.

INDEX

ABOUT THE AUTHOR

Dr. Robert Ball is a Phi Beta Kappa graduate of the University of Kansas, with a masters degree from Princeton Theological Seminary and a masters and a doctorate from San Francisco Theological Seminary. After serving for 28 years as a pastor, he was selected to be the Executive Director of the State of California's Task Force to Promote Self-Esteem, and Personal and Social Responsibility. He has been an adjunct professor for graduate students at San Francisco Theological Seminary and has taught at California State University, Sacramento and various California community colleges. A member of the National Speakers Association, Dr. Ball speaks and gives seminars throughout the United States on subjects related to self-esteem.